March of America Facsimile Series

Number 28

Voyages of Marquette

Jacques Marquette

Voyages of Marquette
in The Jesuit Relations, 59

by Jacques Marquette
With French and English Text

ANN ARBOR

UNIVERSITY MICROFILMS, INC.

A Subsidiary of Xerox Corporation

WINGATE COLLEGE LIBRARY
WINGATE, N. C.

Foreword

These journals of the travels and explorations of the Père
Jacques Marquette, French Jesuit missionary, describe the
arrival of the first Europeans in the upper Mississippi River
Valley. Members of the Jolliet-Marquette expedition of 1673
descended the Mississippi River almost to its point of junc-
tion with the Arkansas River before they turned back. They
established among other things that the Mississippi River
must empty into the Gulf of Mexico rather than into the
Gulf of California. This knowledge profoundly affected the
plans of the French and Spanish governments.

Père Marquette had come to Canada from France in 1666.
In 1672 he was assigned to accompany Louis Jolliet and a
small party to find and to explore "the great river to the
West," i.e., the Mississippi. The party set out in mid-May,
1673. Fear of hostile Indian tribes ahead and fear of capture
by the Spaniards prevented the little band from following
the river all the way to its mouth, however. For Marquette,
the primary purpose of the trip was to save souls. Though
he confessed that he did not know whether the Indians
"apprehended what I told them about God and about matters pertaining to their salvation," yet he remained con-
vinced that "had this voyage resulted in the salvation of
even one soul" he would consider all his trouble well rewarded. Two years after this expedition, Marquette died on
another of his missionary trips near the site of what is today
Ludington, Michigan.

The principal focus of the Marquette journals is religious. Nevertheless, they contain abundant information about the nature of the country and about the customs and mode of life of the Indians. In recent years a controversy has arisen, however, about the authenticity of the journals. Some argue that the journal describing the expedition of 1673 was actually written by Louis Jolliet, not Marquette. According to this theory, Marquette's superior at Quebec, the Père Dablon, secured a copy of Jolliet's journal and reworked it to make Marquette appear to be the author, thinking in this way to glorify Jesuit achievement in New France. Whether Marquette or Jolliet actually wrote the original journal, certainly the Père Dablon seems to have edited it. The journal found its way into print for the first time in 1681, when Thévenot, who evidently had Jesuit contacts in Paris, obtained a copy and inserted it in his *Recueil de voyages*. Through Thévenot, the general public thus learned of the significant results of the Marquette-Jolliet explorations. Publication of the unfinished journal concerning the last period of Marquette's life waited until the nineteenth century. According to one recent student of Marquette, this latter journal is a nineteenth-century fabrication which was intended to enhance Marquette's prestige still further.

The present edition of 1900 includes several seventeenth-century maps showing the penetration of Marquette and Jolliet in the Mississippi Valley. The controversy about the Marquette journals can be studied in detail in Francis B. Steck, *Marquette Legends* (New York, 1960), pp. 71-244, and in Jean Delanglez, *Life and Voyages of Louis Jolliet* (Chicago, 1948), pp. 44-99.

Voyages of Marquette

JACQUES MARQUETTE, S.J.

[From photograph of statue by Sig. Gaetano Trentanove (of Florence, Italy),
which represents Wisconsin in Statuary Hall in the Capitol at Washington.]

The Jesuit Relations and Allied Documents

Travels and Explorations of the Jesuit Missionaries in New France

1610-1791

THE ORIGINAL FRENCH, LATIN, AND ITAL-
IAN TEXTS, WITH ENGLISH TRANSLA-
TIONS AND NOTES; ILLUSTRATED BY
PORTRAITS, MAPS, AND FACSIMILES

EDITED BY

REUBEN GOLD THWAITES

Secretary of the State Historical Society of Wisconsin

Vol. LIX

LOWER CANADA, ILLINOIS, OTTAWAS

1673 – 1677

CLEVELAND: The Burrows Brothers
Company, PUBLISHERS, M DCCCC

CXXXVI—CXXXVIII

VOYAGES DU P. JACQUES MARQUETTE,
1673-75

CXXXVI.—Le premier Voÿage qu'a fait le P. Marquette vers le nouueau Mexique; [Baye des Puants, 1674]

CXXXVII.—Journal incomplet, adressé au R. P. Dablon; n.p., [1675]

CXXXVIII.—Recit du second voyage et de la mort du P. Jacques Marquette; [Quebec, 1677]

SOURCES: These documents are published by us from the original MSS. by Marquette and Dablon, which rest in the archives of St. Mary's College, Montreal.

Le premier Voÿage qu'a fait Le P. Marquette vers le nouueau Mexique & Comment s'en est formé le defsein.

I L y auoit longtemps que le Pere premeditoit Cette Entreprise, porté d'un tres ardent desir d'estendre le Royaume de J. Ch. et de le faire Connoistre et adorer par tous les peuples de ce paÿs. Il se voioit Comme a la porte de ces nouuelles Nations, lorsque dés l'année 1670 il trauailloit en la Mifsion de la pointe du s^t. Esprit qui est a l'extremité du lac superieur aux outaoüacs, il voioit mesme quelquefois plusieurs, de ces nouueaux peuples, desquels il prenoit toutes les Connoissances qu'il pouuoit, c'est ce qui luy a fait faire plusieurs efforts pour commencer cette entreprise, mais tousiour inutilement, et mesme il auoit perdu l esperance d'en venir about lorsque Dieu luy en fit naistre cette occasion.

En L'année 1673 M^r. Le Compte De Frontenac Nostre Gouuerneur, et M^r. Talon alors Nostre Intendant, Connoissant L'Importance de cette découuerte, soit pour chercher vn passage d'icy jusqua la mer de la Chine, par la riuiere qui se décharge a la Mer Vermeille ou Californie, soit qu'on voulu s'asseurer de ce qu'on a dit du depuis, touchant les 2 Roÿaumes le Theguaÿo Et de Quiuira, Limitrophes du Canada, ou l'on tient que les mines d'or sont abondantes, ces Messieurs, dis-ie, nommerent en mesme temps pour Cette entreprise Le Sieur Jolyet quils jugerent tres

Of the first Voyage made by Father Marquette toward new Mexico, and How the idea thereof was conceived.

THE Father had long premeditated This Under-taking, influenced by a most ardent desire to extend the Kingdom of Jesus Christ, and to make him Known and adored by all the peoples of that country. He saw himself, As it were, at the door of these new Nations when, as early as the year 1670, he was laboring in the Mission at the point of st. Esprit, at the extremity of lake superior, among the outaouacs; he even saw occasionally various persons belonging to these new peoples, from whom he obtained all the Information that he could. This induced him to make several efforts to commence this undertaking, but ever in vain; and he even lost all hope of succeeding therein, when God brought about for him the following opportunity.

In The year 1673, Monsieur The Count De Frontenac, Our Governor, and Monsieur Talon, then Our Intendant, Recognizing The Importance of this discovery,— either that they might seek a passage from here to the sea of China, by the river that discharges into the Vermillion, or California Sea; or because they desired to verify what has for some time been said concerning the 2 Kingdoms of Theguaio And Quiuira, which Border on Canada, and in which numerous gold mines are reported to exist,— these Gentlemen, I say, appointed at the same time

propres pour vn si grand dessein, estant bien aise
que Le P. Marquette fut de la partie.

Il ne se tromperent pas dans le choix quils firent
du S^r. Jolyet, Car c'estoit un jeune homme natif de
ce paÿs, qui a pour vn tel dessein tous les aduantages
qu'on peut souhaiter; Il a L'experience, et La
Connoissance des Langues du Paÿs des Outaoüacs, ou
il a passé plusieurs années, il a la Conduitte et la
sagesse qui sont les principales parties pour faire
reussir vn voÿage egalement dangereux et difficile.
Enfin il a le Courage pour ne rien apprehender, ou
tout est a Craindre, aussi a-t-il remplÿ L'attente
qu'on auoit de luy, et si apres auoir passé mille sortes
de dangers, il ne fut venu malheureusement faire
nauffrage au port, son Canot aÿant tourné au dessous
du sault de s^t. Loüys proche de Montreal, ou il a
perdu et ses hommes et ses papiers, et d'ou il n'a
eschapé que par vne espece de Miracle, il ne laissoit
rien a souhaiter au succez de son Voÿage.

SECTION I^{ERE}. DEPART DU P. IACQUES MARQUETTE
POUR L'A DÉCOUUERTE DE LA GRANDE RIUIERE
APPELLÉE PAR LES SAUUAGES MISSISIPI QUI
CONDUIT AU NOUUEAU MEXIQUE.

L E jour de L'IMMACULÉE CONCEPTION de la S^{TE}.
VIERGE, que I'auois tousjour Inuoquée depuisque
je suis en ce paÿs des outaoüacs, pour obtenir de Dieu
la grace de pouuoir visiter les Nations qui sont sur
la Riuiere de Missis[i]pi, fut justement Celuy auquel
arriua M^r. Jollyet auec les ordres de M^r. le Comte de
frontenac Nostre Gouuerneur et de M^r. Talon Nostre
Intendant, pour faire auec moy Cette decouuerte. Je
fus d'autant plus rauy de Cette bonne nouuelle, que
je voiois que mes desseins alloient étre accomplis, et

for This undertaking Sieur Jolyet, whom they considered very fit for so great an enterprise; and they were well pleased that Father Marquette should be of the party.[15]

They were not mistaken in the choice that they made of Sieur Jolyet, For he is a young man, born in this country, who possesses all the qualifications that could be desired for such an undertaking. He has experience and Knows the Languages spoken in the Country of the Outaouacs, where he has passed several years. He possesses Tact and prudence, which are the chief qualities necessary for the success of a voyage as dangerous as it is difficult. Finally, he has the Courage to dread nothing where everything is to be Feared. Consequently, he has fulfilled all The expectations entertained of him; and if, after having passed through a thousand dangers, he had not unfortunately been wrecked in the very harbor, his Canoe having upset below sault st. Louys, near Montreal,— where he lost both his men and his papers, and whence he escaped only by a sort of Miracle,— nothing would have been left to be desired in the success of his Voyage.

SECTION IST.   DEPARTURE OF FATHER JACQUES
MARQUETTE FOR THE DISCOVERY OF THE GREAT
RIVER CALLED BY THE SAVAGES MISSISIPI,
WHICH LEADS TO NEW MEXICO.

THE feast of The IMMACULATE CONCEPTION of the BLESSED VIRGIN — whom I have always Invoked since I have been in this country of the outaouacs, to obtain from God the grace of being able to visit the Nations who dwell along the Missisipi River — was precisely the Day on which Monsieur Jollyet

que je me trouuois dans une heureuse necessité d'exposer ma vie pour le salut de tous ces peuples, et particulierement pour les Ilinois qui m'auoient prié auec beaucoup d'instance lorsque J'estois a la pointe du st. Esprit de leur porter chez Eux la parole de Dieu. Nous ne fusmes pas long temps a preparer tout nostre Equippage, quoy que nous nous Engageassions en vn voÿage dont nous ne pouuions pas preuoir la durée; Du Bled D'Inde auec quelque viande boucanée, furent toutes nos prouisions, auec lesqu'elles nous nous Embarquammes sur 2 Canotz d'Écorce, Mr. Jollyet et moy, auec 5 hommes, bien resolus a tout faire et a tout souffrir pour une si glorieuse Entreprise.

Ce fut donc Le 17e. jour de may 1673 que nous partîmes de la Mission de st. Ignace a Michilimakinac, ou j'estois pour Lors; La Joÿe que nous auions d'étre choisis pour Cette Expedition, animoit nos Courages et nous rendoit agreables les peines que nous auions a ramer depuis le matin jusqu'au soir; et parceque Nous allions chercher des paÿs Inconnus, Nous apportammes toutes les precautions que nous pûmes, affinque si nostre Entreprise estoit hazardeuse elle ne fut pas temeraire; pour ce suject nous prîmes toutes les Connoissances que nous pumes des sauuages qui auoient frequenté ces endroicts là, et mesme nous tracâmes sur leur raport une Carte de tout ce Nouueau paÿs; nous y fîmes marquer les riuieres, sur lesquelles nous deuions nauiger, les noms des peuples et des lieux par lesquels nous deuions passer, le Cours de la grande Riuiere, et quels rund, deuions tenir quand nous y serions.

Sur tout je mis nostre voyage soubs la protection de la Ste. Vierge Immaculée, luy promettant, que si

arrived with orders from Monsieur the Count de frontenac, Our Governor, and Monsieur Talon, Our Intendant, to accomplish This discovery with me. I was all the more delighted at This good news, since I saw that my plans were about to be accomplished; and since I found myself in the blessed necessity of exposing my life for the salvation of all these peoples, and especially of the Ilinois, who had very urgently entreated me, when I was at the point of st. Esprit, to carry the word of God to Their country.

We were not long in preparing all our Equipment, although we were about to Begin a voyage, the duration of which we could not foresee. Indian Corn, with some smoked meat, constituted all our provisions; with these we Embarked — Monsieur Jollyet and myself, with 5 men — in 2 Bark Canoes, fully resolved to do and suffer everything for so glorious an Undertaking.

Accordingly, on The 17th day of may, 1673, we started from the Mission of st. Ignace at Michilimakinac, where I Then was. The Joy that we felt at being selected for This Expedition animated our Courage, and rendered the labor of paddling from morning to night agreeable to us. And because We were going to seek Unknown countries, We took every precaution in our power, so that, if our Undertaking were hazardous, it should not be foolhardy. To that end, we obtained all the Information that we could from the savages who had frequented those regions; and we even traced out from their reports a Map of the whole of that New country; on it we indicated the rivers which we were to navigate, the names of the peoples and of the places through

elle nous faisoit la grace de découurir la grande
Riuiere, Je luy donnerois Le Nom de la Conception
et que je ferois aussi porter ce nom a la premiere
Mission que j'établyrois chez Ces Nouueaux peuples,
ce que jay fait de vraÿ chez les Ilinois.

SECTION 2DE. LE PERE VISITE EN PASSANT LES PEU-
PLES DE LA FOLLE AUOINE, CE QUE C'EST QUE
CETTE FOLLE AUOINE, IL ENTRE DANS LA BAŸE
DES PUANTS, QUELQUES PARTICULARITÉZ DE
CETTE BAŸE, IL ARRIUE A LA NATION DU FEU.

AUEC toutes ces precautions nous faisons Joüer
Joÿeusement les auirons, sur vne partie du Lac
huron et Celuy des Ilinois, et dans la baÿe des
Puants.

La premiere Nation que nous rencontrâmes, fut
Celle de la folle auoine, J'entray dans Leur riuiere,
pour aller visiter ces peuples ausquels nous auons
presché L'Euangile depuis plusieurs années, aussi
se trouve-t-il parmy Eux plusieurs bons chrestiens.

La folle auoine dont ils portent le nom, parcequelle
se trouve sur leurs terres est une sorte d'herbe qui
croit naturellement dans les petites Riuieres dont le
fond est de vase, est dans les Lieux Marescageux;
elle est bien semblable a la folle auoine qui Croit
parmy nos bleds. Les epics sont sur des tuÿeaux
noüés d'Espace en Espace, ils sortent de l Eau vers
le mois de Juin, et vont tousjour montant jusqu'a ce
qu'ils surnagent de deux pieds Enuiron, Le grain
n'est pas plus gros que Celuy de nos auoines, mais il
est vne fois plus long, aussi La farine en est t-elle
bien plus abondante. Voicy Comme les Sauuages la
Cueillent et la preparent pour la manger. Dans Le
mois de Septembre qui est le temps propre pour

which we were to pass, the Course of the great
River, and the direction we were to follow when
we reached it.

Above all, I placed our voyage under the protection of the Blessed Virgin Immaculate, promising
her that, if she granted us the favor of discovering
the great River, I would give it The Name of the
Conception, and that I would also make the first
Mission that I should establish among Those New
peoples, bear the same name.   This I have actually
done, among the Ilinois.[16]

SECTION 2ND.   THE FATHER VISITS, IN PASSING, THE
   TRIBES   OF   THE   FOLLE   AVOINE.   WHAT   THAT
   FOLLE   AVOINE   IS.   HE   ENTERS   THE   BAY   DES
   PUANTS; SOME PARTICULARS ABOUT THAT BAY.
   HE   ARRIVES   AMONG   THE   FIRE   NATION.

WITH all these precautions, we Joyfully Plied our
      paddles on a portion of Lake huron, on That
of the Ilinois and on the bay des Puants.

The first Nation that we came to was That of the
folle avoine.   I entered Their river, to go and visit
these peoples to whom we have preached The Gospel
for several years,— in consequence of which, there
are several good christians among Them.

The wild oat, whose name they bear because it is
found in their country, is a sort of grass, which
grows naturally in the small Rivers with muddy
bottoms, and in Swampy Places.   It greatly resembles the wild oats that Grow amid our wheat.   The
ears grow upon hollow stems, jointed at Intervals;
they emerge from the Water about the month of
June, and continue growing until they rise About
two feet above it.   The grain is not larger than That

Cette recolte, ils vont en Canot autrauers de Ces champs de folle auoine, ils en secoüent les Épics de part et d'autre dans le Canot, a mesure quils auancent le grain tombe aisément s'il est meur, et En peu de temps ils en font leur prouision: Mais pour le net-toÿer de la paille et le dépouiller d'une pellicule dans laquelle il est Enfermé; ils le mettent sécher a la fumée; sur vn gril de bois soubs lequel ils entre-tiennent vn petit feu, pendant quelques Jours, Et lorsque L'auoine est bien seche, ils la mettent dans une Peau en forme de pouche, Laquelle ils enfoncent dans vn trou fait a Ce dessein en terre, puis ils l'a pillent auec les pieds, tant et si fortement que La grain s'estant separé de la paille, ils le vannent tres aisement, apres quoy ils le pillent pour le reduire en farine, ou mesme sans estre pillé ils le font Cuire dans l'eau, qu'ils assaisonnent auec de la graisse, et de Cette façon on trouue La folle auoine presque aussi delicate, qu'est le ris, quand on n'y mette pas de meillieur assaisonnement.

Je racontay a ces peuples de la folle auoine, Le dessein que j auois d'aller découurir Ces nations Esloignées pour les pouuoir Instruire des Mysteres de Nostre S^te. Religion; Ils en furent Extremement surpris, et firent tous leur possible pour m'en dissüa-der; Ils me representerent que je rencontrerois des Nations qui ne pardonnent jamais aux Estrangers ausqu'els ils Cassent La teste sans aucun sujet; que La guerre qui estoit allumée Entre Diuers peuples qui estoient sur nostre Route, nous Exposoit a vn autre danger manifeste d'estre tuéz par les bandes de Guerriers qui sont tousjours en Campagne; que la grande Riuiere est tres dangereuse, quand on n'en scait pas les Endroictz difficiles, qu'elle estoit pleine

of our oats, but it is twice as long, and The meal
therefrom is much more abundant. The Savages
Gather and prepare it for food as Follows. In The
month of September, which is the suitable time for
The harvest, they go in Canoes through These fields
of wild oats; they shake its Ears into the Canoe, on
both sides, as they pass through. The grain falls
out easily, if it be ripe, and they obtain their supply
In a short time. But, in order to clean it from the
straw, and to remove it from a husk in which it is
Enclosed, they dry it in the smoke, upon a wooden
grating, under which they maintain a slow fire for
some Days. When The oats are thoroughly dry,
they put them in a Skin made into a bag, thrust It
into a hole dug in the ground for This purpose, and
tread it with their feet — so long and so vigorously
that The grain separates from the straw, and is very
easily winnowed. After this, they pound it to
reduce it to flour,— or even, without pounding it,
they Boil it in water, and season it with fat. Cooked
in This fashion, The wild oats have almost as delicate a taste as rice has when no better seasoning is
added.

I told these peoples of the folle avoine of My
design to go and discover Those Remote nations, in
order to Teach them the Mysteries of Our Holy
Religion. They were Greatly surprised to hear it,
and did their best to dissuade me. They repre-
sented to me that I would meet Nations who never
show mercy to Strangers, but Break Their heads without any cause; and that war was kindled Between
Various peoples who dwelt upon our Route, which
Exposed us to the further manifest danger of being
killed by the bands of Warriors who are ever in the

de monstres effroÿables, qui deuoroient les hommes et
les Canotz tout Ensemble; qu'il y a mesme vn démon
qu'on entend de fort loing qui en ferme le passage
et qui abysme ceux qui osent en approcher, Enfin que
les Chaleurs sont si excessiues En ces paÿs La
qu'elles nous Causeroient La mort Infailliblement.
Je les remerciay de ces bons aduis qu'ils me don-
noît, mais je leurs dis que je ne pouuois pas les
suiure, puis qu'il s'agissoit du salut des ames pour
lesquelles ie serois rauÿ de donner ma vie, que je
me moquois de ce demon pretendu, que nous nous
deffenderions bien de ces monstres marins, et qu'au
reste Nous Nous tienderions sur nos gardes pour
euiter les autres dangers donts ils nous menaçoient.
Apres les auoir fait prier Dieu et leur auoir donné
quelque Instruction, Je me separaÿ d'eux, et nous
estant Embarquez sur nos Canotz, Nous arriuâmes
peu de temps apres dans le fond de la Baÿe des
puantz, ou nos Peres trauaillent utilement a la
Conuersion de ces peuples, en ayant baptisé plus de
deux mille depuis qu'ils y sont.
Cette baÿe porte vn Nom qui n'a pas une si mauuaise signification en la langue des sauuages, Car ils
l'appellent plustost la baÿe sallée que la Baÿe des
Puans, quoyque parmy Eux ce soit presque le mesme;
& c'est aussi Le nom qu'ils donnent a la Mer;
Ce qui nous a fait faire de tres exactes recherches
pour découurir s'il n'y auoit pas en Ces quartiers
quelques fontaines d'Eau sallée, Comme il y en a
parmy les hiroquois; mais nous n'en auons point
trouué. Nous jugeons donc qu'on luy a donné Ce
nom a cause de quantité de vase et de Boüe qui
s'y rencontre, d'ou s'esleuent Continuellement de
meschantes vapeurs qui y Causent les plus grands

Field. They also said that the great River was very
dangerous, when one does not know the difficult
Places; that it was full of horrible monsters, which
devoured men and Canoes Together; that there was
even a demon, who was heard from a great distance,
who barred the way, and swallowed up all who ven-
tured to approach him; Finally that the Heat was so
excessive In those countries that it would Inevitably
Cause Our death.

I thanked them for the good advice that they gave
me, but told them that I could not follow it, because
the salvation of souls was at stake, for which I would
be delighted to give my life; that I scoffed at the
alleged demon; that we would easily defend ourselves against those marine monsters; and, moreover,
that We would be on our guard to avoid the other
dangers with which they threatened us. After making them pray to God, and giving them some Instruction, I separated from them. Embarking then in
our Canoes, We arrived shortly afterward at the bottom of the Bay des puantz, where our Fathers labor
successfully for the Conversion of these peoples, over
two thousand of whom they have baptized while
they have been there.

This bay bears a Name which has a meaning not
so offensive in the language of the savages; For they
call it *la baye sallée* [" salt bay "] rather than
Bay des Puans,—although with Them this is almost
the same and this is also The name which they give
to the Sea. This led us to make very careful re-
searches to ascertain whether there were not some
salt-Water springs in This quarter, As there are
among the hiroquois, but we found none. We con-
clude, therefore, that This name has been given to

et les plus Continuels Tonnerres, que jaye iamais
entendu.

La Baye a enuiron trente lieuës de profondeur et
huict de large en son Commencement; elle va tousjour se retrécissant jusques dans le fond, ou il est
aisé de remarquer la marée qui a son flux et reflux
reglé presque Comme Celuy de la Mer. Ce n'est
pas icy le lieu d'examiner si ce sont les vrayës ma-
rées, si elles sont Causées par les ventz ou par qu'el-
qu'autre principe, s'il y a des ventz qui sont Les
auantcoureurs de la Lune et attachez a sa suitte lesquels par consequent agitent le lac et luy donnent
Comme son flux et reflux toutes les fois que la Lune
monte sur l'horison. Ce que je peux dire de Certain
est que quand l'eau est bien Calme, on la voit aisement
monter et descendre suivant le Cours de la lune, quoyque je ne nie pas que Ce mouuement ne puisse estre
Causé par les Ventz qui sont bien Eloignez, et qui
pesant sur le milieu du lac font que les bords Croissent
et decroissent de la façon qui paroit a nos yeux.

Nous quittâmes Cette baye pour entrer dans la
riuiere qui s'y décharge; elle est tres belle en son
Emboucheure, et coule doucement, elle est pleine
D'outardes, de Canards de Cercelles et d autres
oyseaux qui y sont attirez par la folle auoine, dont
ils sont fort friants, mais quand on a vn peu auancé
dans cette riuiere, on la trouue tres difficile, tant a
cause des Courants que des Roches affilées, qui Couppent les Canotz et les pieds de Ceux qui sont obligés
de les traisner, sur tout quand les Eaux sont basses.
Nous franchîmes pourtant heureusement Ces rapides
et en approchant de Machkoutens la Nation du feu,
jeu la Curiosité de boire des Eaux mineralles de la
Riuiere qui n'est pas Loing de Cette bourgade, Je

it on account of the quantity of mire and Mud which is seen there, whence noisome vapors Constantly arise, Causing the loudest and most Continual Thunder that I have ever heard.

The Bay is about thirty leagues in depth and eight in width at its Mouth; it narrows gradually to the bottom, where it is easy to observe a tide which has its regular ebb and flow, almost Like That of the Sea. This is not the place to inquire whether these are real tides; whether they are Due to the wind, or to some other cause; whether there are winds, The precursors of the Moon and attached to her suite, which consequently agitate the lake and give it an apparent ebb and flow whenever the Moon ascends above the horizon. What I can Positively state is, that, when the water is very Calm, it is easy to observe it rising and falling according to the Course of the moon; although I do not deny that This movement may be Caused by very Remote Winds, which, pressing on the middle of the lake, cause the edges to Rise and fall in the manner which is visible to our eyes.[17]

We left This bay to enter the river that discharges into it; it is very beautiful at its Mouth, and flows gently; it is full Of bustards, Ducks, Teal, and other birds, attracted thither by the wild oats, of which they are very fond. But, after ascending the river a short distance, it becomes very difficult of passage, on account of both the Currents and the sharp Rocks, which Cut the Canoes and the feet of Those who are obliged to drag them, especially when the Waters are low. Nevertheless, we successfully passed Those rapids; and on approaching Machkoutens, the fire Nation, I had the Curiosity to drink the mineral

pris aussi le temps de reconnoistre vn simple qu'un
sauuage qui en scait le secret a enseigné au P.
Alloües auec beaucoup de Ceremonies, Sa racine sert
Contre la morsure des serpents, Dieu ayant voulu
donner ce remede Contre vn venin qui est tres fre-
quent en ces paÿs: Elle est fort chaude et elle a vn
goust de poudre quand on l'escrase sous la dent; il
faut la mascher et la mettre sur la piquure du serpent, qui en a vne si grande horreur; qu'il s'enfuit
mesme de Celuy qui s'en est frotté, elle produit plusieures tiges hautes d'un pied, dont la feuille est un
peu longue et la fleur blanche et beaucoup semblable
a La giroflée.   J'en mis dans mon Canot, pour l'examiner a loisir, pendant que nous auançions tousjour
vers Maskoutens, ou nous arriuâmes Le 7ᵉ. de Juin.

SECTION 3ᴱᴹᴱ. DESCRIPTION DE LA BOURGADE DE
MASKOUTENS, CE QUI S'Y PASSA ENTRE LE PERE
& LES SAUUAGES; LES FRANÇOIS COMMENCENT
D'ENTRER DANS VN PAŸS NOUUEAU ET
INCONNU ET ARRIUENT A MISSIS[I]PI

NOUS voicy rendus a Maskoutens, ce Mot en Algonquin peut signifier Nation du feu, aussi est
ce le nom qu'on luy a donné; C'est icy le terme des
découuertes qu'on fait les françois, Car ils n'ont point
encor passé plus auant.

Ce Bourg est Composé de trois sortes de Nations
qui s'y sont ramassées, Des Miamis, des Maskoutens,
et des Kikabous les premiers sont les plus ciuils, les
plus liberaux, et les mieux faitz, ils portent deux
longues moustaches sur les oreilles, qui leurs donnent
bonne grace, ils passent pour les guerriers et font
rarement des partis sans succez; ils sont fort dociles,

Waters of the River that is not Far from That village. I also took time to look for a medicinal plant which a savage, who knows its secret, showed to Father Alloues with many Ceremonies. Its root is employed to Counteract snake-bites, God having been pleased to give this antidote Against a poison which is very common in these countries. It is very pungent, and tastes like powder when crushed with the teeth; it must be masticated and placed upon the bite inflicted by the snake. The reptile has so great a horror of it that it even flees from a Person who has rubbed himself with it. The plant bears several stalks, a foot high, with rather long leaves; and a white flower, which greatly resembles The wallflower.[18] I put some in my Canoe, in order to examine it at leisure while we continued to advance toward Maskoutens, where we arrived on The 7th of June.

SECTION 3RD. DESCRIPTION OF THE VILLAGE OF MAS-
KOUTENS; WHAT PASSED THERE BETWEEN THE
FATHER AND THE SAVAGES. THE FRENCH
BEGIN TO ENTER A NEW AND UNKNOWN
COUNTRY, AND ARRIVE AT MISSISIPI.

HERE we are at Maskoutens. This Word may, in Algonquin, mean " the fire Nation,"—which, indeed, is the name given to this tribe. Here is the limit of the discoveries which the french have made, For they have not yet gone any farther.

This Village Consists of three Nations who have gathered there — Miamis, Maskoutens, and Kikabous. The former are the most civil, the most liberal, and the most shapely. They wear two long locks over their ears, which give them a pleasing appearance.

ils escoutent paisiblement Ce qu'on Leur dit, & ont
paru si auides d'Entendre Le P. Alloües quand il les
Instruisoit, qu'ils Luy donnoient peu de repos, mesme
pendant la nuict. Les Maskoutens et les Kikabous
sont plus grossiers et semblent estre des paÿsantz en
Comparaison des autres. Comme les Escorces a faire
des Cabannes sont rares en ce pays la, Ils se seruent
de Joncs qui Leur tiennent lieu de murailles et de
Couuertures, mais qui ne les deffendent pas beaucoup
des vents, et bien moins des pluyës quand elles
tombent en abondance. La Commodité de ces sortes
de Cabannes est qu'ils Les mettent en pacquetz et
les portent aisément où ils veulent pendant Le temps
de leur chasse.

Lorsque Je les visitay, je fus extremément Consolé
de veoir vne belle Croix plantée au milieu du bourg
et ornée de plusieurs peaux blanches, de Ceintures
rouges, d'arcs et de flêches, que ces bonnes gens
auoient offertz au grand Manitou, (C'est le nom qu'ils
donnent a Dieu) pour le remercier de ce qu'il auoit
eu pitié D'Eux pendant L'hyuer, Leur donnant une
chasse abondante, Lorsqu'ils apprehendoient Le plus
La famine.

Je pris plaisir de veoir la situation de cette bourgade, Elle est belle et bien diuertissante, Car d'une
Eminence, sur la quelle elle est placée on découure de
toutes parts des prairies a perte de veüe, partagées par
des bocages, ou par des bois de haute futaÿe : La terre
y est tres bonne, et rend beaucoup de bled d'inde, Les
sauuages ramassent quantité de prunes et de raisins
dont on pourroit faire beaucoup de vin si L'on vouloit.

Nous ne fûsmes pas plustost arriués que nous assem-
blâmes les anciens M^r. Jollyet et moy, il leur dit qu'il

They are regarded as warriors, and rarely undertake expeditions without being successful. They are very docile, and listen quietly to What is said to Them; and they appeared so eager to Hear Father Alloues when he Instructed them that they gave Him but little rest, even during the night. The Maskoutens and Kikabous are ruder, and seem peasants in Comparison with the others. As Bark for making Cabins is scarce in this country, They use Rushes; these serve Them for making walls and Roofs, but do not afford them much protection against the winds, and still less against the rains when they fall abundantly. The Advantage of Cabins of this kind is, that they make packages of Them, and easily transport them wherever they wish, while they are hunting.

When I visited them, I was greatly Consoled at seeing a handsome Cross erected in the middle of the village, and adorned with many white skins, red Belts, and bows and arrows, which these good people had offered to the great Manitou (This is the name which they give to God). They did this to thank him for having had pity On Them during The winter, by giving Them an abundance of game When they Most dreaded famine.[19]

I took pleasure in observing the situation of this village. It is beautiful and very pleasing; For, from an Eminence upon which it is placed, one beholds on every side prairies, extending farther than the eye can see, interspersed with groves or with lofty trees. The soil is very fertile, and yields much indian corn. The savages gather quantities of plums and grapes, wherewith much wine could be made, if desired.

estoit enuoyé de la part de Monsr. Nostre Gouuerneur pour découurir de Nouueaus paÿs, et moy de la
part de Dieu pour les Esclairer des lumieres du s^t.
Euangile, qu'au reste Le Maistre souuerain de nos
vies vouloit estre connu de toutes les Nations, et
que pour obéir a ses volontés, je ne craignois pas la
mort a laquelle je m'exposois dans des voyages si
perilleux. Que nous auions besoin de deux guides
pour nous mettre dans nostre route; Nous leur
fîmes un present, en les priant de nous les accorder,
ce qu'ils firent tres Ciuilement et mesme voulurent
aussi nous parler par vn present qui fut une Nate
pour nous seruir de lit pendant tout nostre voÿage.

Le lendemain qui fut le dixiéme de Juin, deux
Miamis qu'on nous donna pour guides s'embarque-
rent auec nous, a la veüe d'un grand monde, qui ne
pouuoit assez s'estonner, de veoir sept françois, seuls,
et dans deux Canotz oser entreprendre une Expedition si extresordinaire et si hazardeuse.

Nous scauions qua trois lieuës de Maskoutens estoit
vne Riuiere qui se décharge dans Missisipi; Nous
scauions encor que le rund de vent que nous deuions
tenir pour y arriuer estoit L'ouest soroüest mais le
chemin est partagé de tant de marais et de petitz
lacs, qu'il est aisé de s'y égarer, d'autant plus que la
Riuiere qui y méne est si chargée de folle auoine,
qu'on a peine a en raconnoistre le Canal, C'est en
quoy nous auions bien besoin de nos deux guides,
aussi nous Conduisirent-ils heureusement jusque vn
portage de 2700 pas, et nous aiderent a transporter
nos Canotz pour entrer dans Cette riuiere, apres quoy
ils s'en retournerent, nous laissant seuls en ce paÿs
Inconnu, entre les mains de la prouidence.

No sooner had we arrived than we, Monsieur
Jollyet and I, assembled the elders together; and
he told them that he was sent by Monsieur Our
Governor to discover New countries, while I was sent
by God to Illumine them with the light of the holy
Gospel.   He told them that, moreover, The sov-
ereign Master of our lives wished to be known by all
the Nations; and that in obeying his will I feared
not the death to which I exposed myself in voyages
so perilous.   He informed them that we needed two
guides to show us the way; and We gave them a
present, by it asking them to grant us the guides.
To this they very Civilly consented; and they also
spoke to us by means of a present, consisting of a
Mat to serve us as a bed during the whole of our
voyage.

On the following day, the tenth of June, two
Miamis who were given us as guides embarked with
us, in the sight of a great crowd, who could not sufficiently express their astonishment at the sight of
seven frenchmen, alone and in two Canoes, daring to
undertake so extraordinary and so hazardous an
Expedition.

We knew that, at three leagues from Maskoutens,
was a River which discharged into Missisipi.   We
knew also that the direction we were to follow in
order to reach it was west-southwesterly.   But the
road is broken by so many swamps and small lakes
that it is easy to lose one's way, especially as the
River leading thither is so full of wild oats that it is
difficult to find the Channel.   For this reason we
greatly needed our two guides, who safely Conducted
us to a portage of 2,700 paces, and helped us to
transport our Canoes to enter That river; after

Nous quittons donc les E:ux qui vont jusqua Quebeq a 4 ou 500 Lieuës d'icy pour prendre Celles qui
nous Conduiront desormais dans des terres estran-
geres. auant que de nous y embarquer, nous Com-
mençâmes tous ensemble une nouuelle deuotion a la
s^te. Vierge Immaculée que nous pratiquâmes tous les
jours, luy addressant des prieres particuliers pour
mettre sous sa protection, et nos personnes et le
succez de nostre voÿage, et apres nous estre encou-
ragés les vns les autres nous montons en Canot.

La Riuiere sur laquelle nous nous embarquâmes
s'appelle Meskousing, elle est fort large, son fond
est du sable, qui fait diuerses battures lesquelles
rendent cette nauigation tres difficile, elle est pleine
d'Isles Couuertes de Vignes; sur les bords parroissent
de bonnes terres, entremeslées de bois de prairies et
de Costeaux, on y voit des chesnes, des Noiers, des
bois blancs, et une autre espece d'arbres dontz les
branches sont armées de longues espines. Nous
n'auons veu ny gibier, ny poisson, mais bien des
cheurëilz et des vaches en assez grande quantité,
nostre Route estoit au suroüest et apres auoir nauigé
enuiron 30 lieuës, nous apperceûmes un endroit qui
auoit toutes les apparences de mine de fer, et de fait
vn de nous qui en a veu autrefois, assure que Celle que
Nous auons trouuée est fort bonne et tres abondante,
elle est Couuerte de trois pieds de bonne terre, assez
proche d'une chaine de rocher, dont le bas est plein
de fort beau bois, apres 40 lieuës sur Cette mesme
route, nous arriuons a l'embouchure de nostre Riuiere
et nous trouuant a 42 degrez et demy D'esleuation,
Nous entrons heureusement dans Missisipi Le 17^e.
Juin auec vne Joÿe que je ne peux pas Expliquer.

which they returned home, leaving us alone in this
Unknown country, in the hands of providence.[20]

Thus we left the Waters flowing to Quebeq, 4 or
500 Leagues from here, to float on Those that would
thenceforward Take us through strange lands. Before embarking thereon, we Began all together a
new devotion to the blessed Virgin Immaculate,
which we practiced daily, addressing to her special
prayers to place under her protection both our
persons and the success of our voyage; and, after
mutually encouraging one another, we entered our
Canoes.

The River on which we embarked is called Meskousing. It is very wide; it has a sandy bottom,
which forms various shoals that render its navigation
very difficult. It is full of Islands Covered with
Vines. On the banks one sees fertile land, diversi-
fied with woods, prairies, and Hills. There are oak,
Walnut, and basswood trees; and another kind,
whose branches are armed with long thorns. We
saw there neither feathered game nor fish, but many
deer, and a large number of cattle. Our Route lay
to the southwest, and, after navigating about 30
leagues, we saw a spot presenting all the appear-
ances of an iron mine; and, in fact, one of our party
who had formerly seen such mines, assures us that
The One which We found is very good and very rich.
It is Covered with three feet of good soil, and is
quite near a chain of rocks, the base of which is covered by very fine trees. After proceeding 40 leagues
on This same route, we arrived at the mouth of our
River; and, at 42 and a half degrees Of latitude, We
safely entered Missisipi on The 17th of June, with a
Joy that I cannot Express.

SECTION 4ᵉᵐᵉ. DE LA GRANDE RIUIERE APPELLÉE
MISSISIPI SES PLUS NOTABLES PARTICULARITÉS, DE
DIUERS ANIMAUX ET PARTICULIEREMENT DES
PISIKIO·JS OU BŒUFS SAUUAGES, LEUR FIGURE
ET LEUR NATUREL, DES PREMIERS VILLAGES
DES ILINOIS OÙ LES FRANÇOIS ARRIUENT.

NOUS voyla donc sur cette Riuiere si renommée
dont iay taché d'en remarquer attentiuement
toutes les singularités; La Riuiere de Missisipi tire
son origine de diuers lacs qui sont dans le paÿs des
peuples du Nord, elle est estroitte a sa décharge de
Miskous; son Courant qui port du Costé du sud est
lent et paisible, a la droitte on voist vne grande
Chaisne de Montagnes fort hautes et a la gauche de
belles terres, elle est Couppée d'Isles en diuers Endroictz; En sondant nous auons trouués dix brasses
d'Eaux, sa Largeur est fort inegale, elle a quelque
fois trois quartz de lieuës et quelquefois elle se
rétressit jusqua trois arpens.   Nous suiuons doucement son Cours, qui va au sud et au sudest jusquaus
42 degrés d'Eleuation.   C'est icy que nous nous
apperceuons bien qu'elle a tout changé de face; Il ny
a presque plus de bois n'y de montagnes, Les Isles
sont plus beles et Couuertes de plus beaux arbres;
Nous ne voions que des cheureils et de vaches, des
outardes et des Cygnes sans aisles, parcequ'ils quit-
tent Leurs plumes en Ce paÿs: Nous rencontrons de
temps en temps des poissons monstrueux, vn desquels
donna si rudement Contre nostre Canot que je Crû
que c'estoit un gros arbre qui L'alloit mettre en
piéces vne autrefois nous apperceûmes sur L'eau vn
monstre qui auoit vne teste de tygre, les néz pointu
Comme Celuy d'un chat sauuage, auec la barbe &
des oreilles droittes Éleuées en haut, La teste estoit

SECTION 4TH. OF THE GREAT RIVER CALLED MISSI-
SIPI; ITS MOST NOTABLE FEATURES; OF VARIOUS
ANIMALS, AND ESPECIALLY THE PISIKIOUS OR
WILD CATTLE, THEIR SHAPE AND NATURE;
OF THE FIRST VILLAGES OF THE ILINOIS,
WHERE   THE   FRENCH   ARRIVED.

HERE we are, then, on this so renowned River, all
of whose peculiar features I have endeavored
to note carefully. The Missisipi River takes its rise
in various lakes in the country of the Northern
nations. It is narrow at the place where Miskous
empties; its Current, which flows southward, is slow
and gentle. To the right is a large Chain of very
high Mountains, and to the left are beautiful lands;
in various Places, the stream is Divided by Islands.
On sounding, we found ten brasses of Water. Its
Width is very unequal; sometimes it is three-quar-
ters of a league, and sometimes it narrows to three
arpents. We gently followed its Course, which runs
toward the south and southeast, as far as the 42nd
degree of Latitude. Here we plainly saw that its
aspect was completely changed. There are hardly
any woods or mountains; The Islands are more beautiful, and are Covered with finer trees. We saw
only deer and cattle, bustards, and Swans without
wings, because they drop Their plumage in This
country. From time to time, we came upon mon-
strous fish, one of which struck our Canoe with such
violence that I Thought that it was a great tree,
about to break the Canoe to pieces.[21] On another
occasion, we saw on The water a monster with the
head of a tiger, a sharp nose Like That of a wildcat,
with whiskers and straight, Erect ears; The head
was gray and The Neck quite black; but We saw no

grize et La Col tout noir, Nous n'en vismes pas
d'auantage.   quand nous auons jetté nos retz a l'eau
nous auons pris des Esturgeons et une Espece de
poisson fort extresordinaire, il ressemble a la truitte
auec Cette difference qu'il a la geule plus grande, il
a proche du nez qui est plus petit aussi bien que les
yeux vne grande Areste faite Comme vn bust de
femme, large de trois doigts, Long d'une Coudée, au
bout de laquelle est vn rond Large Comme la main.
Cela l'oblige souuent en saultant hors de l eau de tomber en derriere.   Estant descendus jusqua 41 degrés
28 minuittes suiuant Le mesme rund, nous trouuons
que les Coqs d'inde ont pris la place du gibier, et les
pisikious ou bœufs sauuages, Celle des autres bestes.

Nous les appelons bœufs sauuages parcequ'ils sont
bien semblables a nos bœufs domestiques, ils ne sont
pas plus longs mais ils sont pres d'une fois plus gros
et plus Corpulentz; Nos gens en ayant tué vn trois
personnes auoient bien de la peine a le remüer, ils
ont la teste fort grosse, Le front plat et Large d'un
pied et demy entre les Cornes qui sont entierement
semblables a Celles de nos bœufs, mais elles sont
noires et beaucoup plus grande, Ils ont sous le Col
Comme vne grande falle, qui pend en bas et sur Le
dos vne bosse assez éleuée.   Toute la teste, Le Col,
et une partie des Espaules sont Couuertez d'un grand
Crin Comme Celuy des cheuaux, C'est une hûre
longue d'un pied, qui les rend hideux et leur tombant
sur les yeux les Empéche de voire deuant Eux; Le
reste du Corps est reuetu d'un gros poil frisé a peu
pres Cõme Celuy de nos moutons, mais bien plus
fort et plus Espais, il tombe en Esté et La peau
deuient douce Comme du Velours. C'est pourlors
que les sauuages les Emploÿent pour s'en faire de

more creatures of this sort.   When we cast our nets
into the water we caught Sturgeon, and a very extraordinary Kind of fish.   It resembles the trout, with
This difference, that its mouth is larger.   Near its
nose — which is smaller, as are also the eyes — is a
large Bone shaped Like a woman's busk, three fingers wide and a Cubit Long, at the end of which is
a disk as Wide As one's hand.   This frequently
causes it to fall backward when it leaps out of
the water.[20]   When we reached the parallel of 41
degrees 28 minutes, following The same direction, we
found that Turkeys had taken the place of game;
and the pisikious, or wild cattle, That of the other
animals.

We call them " wild cattle," because they are very
similar to our domestic cattle.   They are not longer,
but are nearly as large again, and more Corpulent.
When Our people killed one, three persons had much
difficulty in moving it.   The head is very large;
The forehead is flat, and a foot and a half Wide between the Horns, which are exactly like Those of our
oxen, but black and much larger.   Under the Neck
They have a Sort of large dewlap, which hangs down;
and on The back is a rather high hump.   The whole
of the head, The Neck, and a portion of the Shoul-
ders, are Covered with a thick Mane Like That of
horses; It forms a crest a foot long, which makes
them hideous, and, falling over their eyes, Prevents
them from seeing what is before Them.   The
remainder of the Body is covered with a heavy coat
of curly hair, almost Like That of our sheep, but
much stronger and Thicker.   It falls off in Summer,
and The skin becomes as soft As Velvet.   At that
season, the savages Use the hides for making fine

belles Robbes qu'ils peignent de diuerses Couleurs;
la chair et la graisse des pisikious est Excellente et
fait le meillieur mets des festins au reste ils sont tres
méchants et il ne se passent point d'année qu'ils ne
tuent quelques sauuages quand on vient les attaquer,
ils prennent s'ils peuuent un homme auec leurs
Cornes, L'enleuent en l'air puis ils le jettent contre
terre, le foulent des pieds et le tuent, si on tire de
loing sur Eux ou de larc ou du fusil, il faut si tost
apres le Coup se jetter a terre et se cacher dans
l'herbe, Car s'ils apercoiuent Celuy qui a tiré, ils
Courent apres et le vont attaquer,   Comme ils ont les
pieds gros et assez Courtz ils ne vont pas bien viste
pour l'ordinaire, si ce n'est lorsqu'ils sont irritez.
Ils sont espars dans les prairies Comme des trou-
peaux j'en ay veu vne bande de 400.

Nous auancons tousjours mais Comme nous ne
scauions pas où nous allions ayant fait déia plus de
Cent lieuës sans auoir rien découuert que des bestes
et des oÿseaux nous Nous tenons bien sur nos gardes;
C'est pourquoy nous ne faisons qu'un petit feu a terre
sur le soir pour preparer nos repas, et apres soûper
nous Nous en eloignons le plus que nous pouuons, et
nous allons passer la nuict dans nos Canotz que nous
tenons a l'ancre sur la riuiere asséz loing des bords;
Ce qui n'empéche pas que qu'elquun de nous ne
soit tousjour en sentinelle de peur de surprise, allant
par le sud et le sud suroüest nous nous trouuons a
la hauteur de 41 degréz et jusqua 40 degrez quelques
minutes en partie par sudest et en partie par le suroüest.   Apres auoir auancé plus de 60 lieües depuis
Nostre Entrée dans la Riuiere sans rien découurir.

Enfin le 25ᵉ. Juin nous aperceûmes sur le bord de
leau des pistes d'hommes, et un petit sentier asséz

Robes, which they paint in various Colors. The flesh and the fat of the pisikious are Excellent, and constitute the best dish at feasts. Moreover, they are very fierce; and not a year passes without their killing some savages. When attacked, they catch a man on their Horns, if they can, toss Him in the air, and then throw him on the ground, after which they trample him under foot, and kill him. If a person fire at Them from a distance, with either a bow or a gun, he must, immediately after the Shot, throw himself down and hide in the grass; For if they perceive Him who has fired, they Run at him, and attack him. As their legs are thick and rather Short, they do not run very fast, As a rule, except when angry. They are scattered about the prairie in herds; I have seen one of 400.

We continued to advance, but, As we knew not whither we were going,—for we had proceeded over one Hundred leagues without discovering anything except animals and birds,—we kept well on our guard. On this account, we make only a small fire on land, toward evening, to cook our meals; and, after supper, we remove Ourselves as far from it as possible, and pass the night in our Canoes, which we anchor in the river at some distance from the shore. This does not prevent us from always posting one of the party as a sentinel, for fear of a surprise. Proceeding still in a southerly and south-southwesterly direction, we find ourselves at the parallel of 41 degrees, and as low as 40 degrees and some minutes,— partly southeast and partly southwest,—after having advanced over 60 leagues since We Entered the River, without discovering anything.

Finally, on the 25th of June, we perceived on the

battu qui entroit dans une belle prairie. Nous Nous
arrestâmes pour l'Examiner, et jugeant que cestoit
un chemin qui Conduisoit a quelque village de sauuages, Nous prîmes resolution de l'aller reconnoistre;
nous laissons donc nos deux Canotz sous la garde de
nos gens, Leur recommandant bien de ne se pas
laisser surprendre, apres quoy M^r. Jollyet et moy
entreprîmes cette découuerte asséz hazardeuse pour
deux hommes seuls qui s'exposent a la discretion
d'un peuple barbare et Inconnu. Nous suiuons en
silence. Ce petit sentier, et apres auoir fait Enuiron
2 lieuës, Nous découurîmes vn village sur le bord
d'une riuiere, et deux autres sur vn Costeau escarté
du premier d'une demi lieüe, Ce fut pour lors que
nous nous recommandâmes a Dieu de bon Cœur, et
ayant imploré son secours, nous passâmes outre sans
être découuerts et nous vinsmes si près que nous
entendions mesme parler les sauuages. Nous Crûmes
donc qu'il estoit temps de nous découurir, ce que
Nous fismes par vn Cry que nous poussâmes de
toutes Nos forces, en nous arrestant sans plus avancer.   A ce cry les sauuages sortent promptement de
leurs Cabanes Et nous ayant probablement reconnus
pour françois, sur tout voÿant une robe noire, ou du
moins n'ayant aucun suject de deffiance, puisque
nous n'estions que deux hommes, et que nous les
auions aduertis de nostre arriuée, ils députerent
quatre vielliards, pour nous venir parler, dontz deux
portoient des pipes a prendre du tabac, bien ornées
et Empanachées de diuers plumages, ils marchoient
a petit pas, et éleuant leurs pipes vers le soleil, ils
sembloient luy presenter a fumer, sans neamoins
dire aucun mot. Ils furent assez longtemps a faire
le peu de chemin depuis leur village jusqu'a nous.

water's edge some tracks of men, and a narrow and
somewhat beaten path leading to a fine prairie. We
stopped to Examine it; and, thinking that it was a
road which Led to some village of savages, We
resolved to go and reconnoiter it. We therefore left
our two Canoes under the guard of our people,
strictly charging Them not to allow themselves to
be surprised, after which Monsieur Jollyet and I
undertook this investigation — a rather hazardous one
for two men who exposed themselves, alone, to the
mercy of a barbarous and Unknown people. We
silently followed The narrow path, and, after walking About 2 leagues, We discovered a village on the
bank of a river, and two others on a Hill distant
about half a league from the first.[28] Then we
Heartily commended ourselves to God, and, after
imploring his aid, we went farther without being
perceived, and approached so near that we could
even hear the savages talking. We therefore Decided that it was time to reveal ourselves. This We
did by Shouting with all Our energy, and stopped,
without advancing any farther. On hearing the
shout, the savages quickly issued from their Cabins,
And having probably recognized us as frenchmen,
especially when they saw a black gown,— or, at
least, having no cause for distrust, as we were only
two men, and had given them notice of our arrival,—
they deputed four old men to come and speak to us.
Two of these bore tobacco-pipes, finely ornamented
and Adorned with various feathers. They walked
slowly, and raised their pipes toward the sun, seem-
ingly offering them to it to smoke,— without, however, saying a word. They spent a rather long time
in covering the short distance between their village

Enfin nous ayant abordés, ils s'arresterent pour nous
Considerer auec attention; Je me r'assuray, voyant
ces Ceremoniës qui ne se font parmy eux qu'entr'-
amys, et bien plus quand je les vis Couuertz d'Estoffe,
jugeant par la qu'ils estoient de nos alliez. Je leurs
parlay donc le premier, et Je leurs demandaÿ qui ils
estoient, ils me répondirent qu'ils estoient Ilinois, et
pour marque de paix ils nous presenterent leurs pipes
pour petuner, Ensuitte ils nous inuiterent d'entrer
dans leur Village, où tout le peuple nous attendoit
auec impatience. Ces pipes a prendre du tabac s'appellent en Ce paÿs des Calumetz; ce mot s'y est mit
tellement En vsage que pour estre entendu je seraÿ
obligé de m'en seruir ayant a en parler bien des fois.

SECTION 5ᴱ. COMMENT LES ILINOIS RECEURENT LE
PERE DANS LEUR BOURGADE

A LA Porte de la Cabane où nous deuions estre
receus, estoit un vielliard qui nous attendoit
dans une posture assez surprenante qui est la Ceremonie qu'ils gardent quand ils recoiuent des Estrangers. Cet homme estoit debout et tout nud, tenant
ses mains estendus et leuées vers le soleil, Comme
s'il eut voulu se deffendre de ses raÿons, lesquels
neamoins passoient sur son visage entre ses doigts;
quand nous fusmes proches de luy il nous fit Ce
Compliment; Que le soleil est beau, françois, quand
tu nous viens uisiter, tout nostre bourg t'attend, et
tu entreras en paix dans toute nos Cabanes. Cela
dit, il nous introduisit, dans la sienne, où il y auoit
vne foule de monde qui nous deuoroit des yeux, qui
cependant gardoit un profond silence, on entendoit
neamoins ces paroles qu'on nous addressoit de temps

and us. Finally, when they had drawn near, they
stopped to Consider us attentively. I was reassured
when I observed these Ceremonies, which with them
are performed only among friends; and much more
so when I saw them Clad in Cloth, for I judged
thereby that they were our allies. I therefore spoke
to them first, and asked them who they were. They
replied that they were Ilinois; and, as a token of
peace, they offered us their pipes to smoke. They
afterward invited us to enter their Village, where
all the people impatiently awaited us. These pipes
for smoking tobacco are called in This country
Calumets. This word has come so much Into use
that, in order to be understood, I shall be obliged to
use it, as I shall often have to mention these pipes.

SECTION 5TH.   HOW THE ILINOIS RECEIVED THE
FATHER IN THEIR VILLAGE.

A T the Door of the Cabin in which we were to be
received was an old man, who awaited us in a
rather surprising attitude, which constitutes a part
of the Ceremonial that they observe when they
receive Strangers. This man stood erect, and stark
naked, with his hands extended and lifted toward the
sun, As if he wished to protect himself from its rays,
which nevertheless shone upon his face through his
fingers. When we came near him, he paid us This
Compliment: "How beautiful the sun is, O frenchman, when thou comest to visit us! All our village
awaits thee, and thou shalt enter all our Cabins in
peace." Having said this, he made us enter his own,
in which were a crowd of people; they devoured us
with their eyes, but, nevertheless, observed profound
silence. We could, however, hear these words,

en temps et d'une voix basse, que voyla qui est bien,
Mes freres de ce que vous nous visitez.

Apres que Nous eusmes pris place, on nous fit la
Ciuilité ordinaire du paÿs, qui est de nous presenter le
Calumet, il ne faut pas le refuser, si on ne veut passer
pour Ennemy où dumoins pour inciuil, pourueu qu'on
fasse semblant de fumer c'est assez; pendant que tous
les anciens petunoient apres Nous pour nous honorer,
on vient nous inuiter de la part du grand Capitaine de
tous les Ilinois de nous transporter en sa Bourgade,
ou il vouloit tenir Conseil auec nous. Nous y allâmes
en bonne Compagnie. Car tous ces peuples qui
n'auoient jamais veu de françois chez Eux ne se
lassoient point de nous regarder, ils se Couchoient
sur L'herbe le long des chemins, ils nous deuançoient,
puis ils retournoient sur leurs pas, pour nous venir
voir Encore   Tout cela se faisoit sans bruit et auec les
marques d'un grand respect qu'ils auoient pour nous.

Estant arriuez au Bourg du grand Capitaine, Nous
le vismes a l'entrée de sa Cabanne, au milieu de deux
vielliards, tous trois debout et nud tenant leur
Calumet tourné vers le soleil,   il nous harangua En
peu de motz, nous felicitant de nostre arriuée, il nous
presenta ensuitte son Calumet et nous fit fumer, en
mesme temps que nous entrions dans sa Cabanne, où
nous receumes toutes leurs Caresses ordinaires.

Voÿant tout le monde assemblé et dans le silence,
Je leur parlay par quattre presents que je leur fis,
par le premier je leur disois que nous marchions en
paix pour uisiter les nations qui estoient sur la
Riuiere jusqu'a la Mer.   par le second je leur decla-
ray, que Dieu qui les a Crées auoit pitié d'Eux,
puis qu'apres tant de temps qu'il l'ont ignoré, il vou-

which were addressed to us from time to time in a
low voice: " How good it is, My brothers, that you
should visit us."

After We had taken our places, the usual Civility
of the country was paid to us, which consisted in
offering us the Calumet.   This must not be refused,
unless one wishes to be considered an Enemy, or at
least uncivil; it suffices that one make a pretense of
smoking.   While all the elders smoked after Us, in
order to do us honor, we received an invitation on
behalf of the great Captain of all the Ilinois to proceed to his Village where he wished to hold a Council with us.   We went thither in a large Company,
For all these people, who had never seen any frenchmen among Them, could not cease looking at us.
They Lay on The grass along the road; they preceded
us, and then retraced their steps to come and see us
Again.   All this was done noiselessly, and with
marks of great respect for us.

When we reached the Village of the great Captain,
We saw him at the entrance of his Cabin, between
two old men,— all three erect and naked, and holding their Calumet turned toward the sun.   He
harangued us In a few words, congratulating us
upon our arrival.   He afterward offered us his Calumet, and made us smoke while we entered his Cabin,
where we received all their usual kind Attentions.

Seeing all assembled and silent, I spoke to them
by four presents that I gave them.   By the first, I
told them that we were journeying peacefully to visit
the nations dwelling on the River as far as the Sea.
By the second, I announced to them that God, who
had Created them, had pity on Them, inasmuch as,
after they had so long been ignorant of him, he

loit se faire Connoistre a tous ces peuples, que j'estois
Enuoyé de sa part pour ce dessein, que c'estoit a Eux
a le reconnoistre et a luy obéir.   Par le troisieme
que le grand Capitaine des françois leur faisoit scauoir, que c'estoit luy qui mettoit la paix partout et
qui auoit dompté L'Iroquois.   Enfin par le quatriéme
nous les prions de nous donner toutes Les Connoissances qu'ils auoient de la Mer, et des Nations par
Lesquelles nous deuions passer pour y arriuer.

Quand jeu finÿ mon discour, le Capitaine se leua,
et tenant La main sur la teste d'un petit Esclaue
qu'il nous vouloit donner il parla ainsi.   Je te remer-
cy Robe Noire, et toy françois s'addressant a Mᵣ.
Jollyet, de ce que vous prenez tant de peine pour
nous venir visiter, jamais la terre n'a esté si belle ny
le soleil si Éclatant qu'aujourd'huy; Jamais nostre
riuiere n'a este si Calme, n'y si nette de rochers que
vos canotz ont Enleuées en passant, jamais nostre
petun n'a eü si bon goust, n'y nos bleds n'ont paru
si beaux que Nous Les voions maintenant.   Voicy
mon fils que je te donne pour te faire Connoistre mon
Cœur, je te prie d'auoir pitié de moy, et de toute
ma Nation,   C'est toy qui Connoist le grand Genie
qui nous a tous faits, C'est toy qui Luy parle et qui
escoute sa parole, demande Luy qu'il me donne la
vie et la santé, et vient demeurer auec nous, pour
nous le faire Connoistre.   Cela dit, il mit le petit
Esclaue proche de nous, et nous fit un second
present, qui estoit un Calumet tout mysterieux, dont
ils font plus d'estat que d'un Esclaue; il nous témoi-
gnoit par ce present L'estime qu'il faisoit de Monsieur Nostre Gouuerneur, sur le recit que nous luy
en auions fait; et pour un troisiéme il nous prioit de

wished to make himself Known to all the peoples; that I was Sent by him for that purpose; and that it was for Them to acknowledge and obey him.   By the third, I said that the great Captain of the French informed them that he it was who restored peace everywhere; and that he had subdued The Iroquois. Finally, by the fourth, we begged them to give us all The Information that they had about the Sea, and about the Nations through Whom we must pass to reach it.

When I had finished my speech, the Captain arose, and, resting His hand upon the head of a little Slave whom he wished to give us, he spoke thus: "I thank thee, Black Gown, and thee, O frenchman,"— addressing himself to Monsieur Jollyet,—"for having taken so much trouble to come to visit us. Never has the earth been so beautiful, or the sun so Bright, as to-day; Never has our river been so Calm, or so clear of rocks, which your canoes have Removed in passing; never has our tobacco tasted so good, or our corn appeared so fine, as We now see Them.   Here is my son, whom I give thee to Show thee my Heart.   I beg thee to have pity on me, and on all my Nation.   It is thou who Knowest the great Spirit who has made us all.   It is thou who speakest to Him, and who hearest his word.   Beg Him to give me life and health, and to come and dwell with us, in order to make us Know him."   Having said this, he placed the little Slave near us, and gave us a second present, consisting of an altogether mysterious Calumet, upon which they place more value than upon a Slave.   By this gift, he expressed to us The esteem that he had for Monsieur Our Governor, from the account which we had given of him; and, by a

la part de toute sa Nation, de ne pas passer oultre, a cause des grands dangers où nous nous Exposions.

Je répondis, que je ne Craignois point La mort, et que je n'estimois point de plus grand bonheur que de perdre la vie pour la gloire de Celuy qui a tout fait. C'est ce que ces pauures peuples ne peuuent Comprendre.

Le Conseil fut suiuÿ d'un grand festin qui Consistoit en quattre metz qu'il fallut prendre auec toutes leurs façons, Le premier seruice fut un grand plat de bois plein de sagamité, cest-a-dire de farine de bled d'inde qu'ont fait boüillir auec de leau qu'on assaisonne de graisse. Le Maistre des Ceremonies auec vne Cueillier pleine de sagamité me la presenta a la bouche par trois ou 4 fois, Comme on feroit a vn petit Enfant, il fit Le mesme a M^r. Jollyet. pour second metz il fit paroistre un second plat où il y auoit trois poissons, il en prit quelques morceaux pour en oster les arestes, et ayant soufflé dessus pour Les rafraichir, il nous les mit a la bouche, Comme L'on donneroit la beschée a un oyseau. on apporte pour troisiéme seruice vn grand chien, qu'on venoit de tuer, mais ayant appris que nous n'en mangions point, on le retira de deuant nous. Enfin le 4e. fut une piéce de bœuf sauuage, dont on nous mit a la bouche Les morceaux les plus gras.

Apres ce festin il fallut aller visiter tout le village qui est bien Composé de 300 Cabannes, pendant que nous marchions par les Rües, vn orateur haranguoit Continuellement pour obliger tout le monde a nous voir sans nous estre Importuns; on nous presentoit partout des Ceintures, des jartieres, et autres ouurages faits de poil d'ours et de bœuf, et tiens en

third, he begged us on behalf of all his Nation not to
go farther, on account of the great dangers to which
we Exposed ourselves.

I replied that I Feared not death, and that I
regarded no happiness as greater than that of losing
my life for the glory of Him who has made all. This
is what these poor people cannot Understand.

The Council was followed by a great feast, Consisting of four dishes, which had to be partaken of
in accordance with all their fashions. The first
course was a great wooden platter full of sagamité,—
that is to say, meal of indian corn boiled in water,
and seasoned with fat. The Master of Ceremonies
filled a Spoon with sagamité three or 4 times, and
put it to my mouth As if I were a little Child. He
did The same to Monsieur Jollyet. As a second
course, he caused a second platter to be brought, on
which were three fish. He took some pieces of
them, removed the bones therefrom, and, after blowing upon them to cool Them, he put them in our
mouths As one would give food to a bird. For the
third course, they brought a large dog, that had just
been killed; but, when they learned that we did not
eat this meat, they removed it from before us.
Finally, the 4th course was a piece of wild ox, The
fattest morsels of which were placed in our mouths.

After this feast, we had to go to visit the whole
village, which Consists of fully 300 Cabins. While
we walked through the Streets, an orator Continually
harangued to oblige all the people to come to see
us without Annoying us. Everywhere we were pre-
sented with Belts, garters, and other articles made
of the hair of bears and cattle, dyed red, Yellow,
and gray. These are all the rarities they possess.

rouge, en Jaune et en gris, Ce sont toutes les raretéz
quils ont Comme elles ne sont pas bien Conside-
rables, nous ne nous En chargeames point.

Nous Couchâmes dans la Cabane du Capitaine, et
le lendemain nous prismes Congé de luy, promettant
de repasser par son bourg dans quatre lunes. Il
nous Conduisit jusqua nos Canotz auec pres de 600
personnes, qui nous virent Embarquer, nous donnant toutes les marques qu'ils pouuoient de la joÿe
que Nostre visite leur auoit causée. Je m'engageaÿ
en mon particulier, en leur disant a Dieu que je vien-
drois l'an prochain demeurer auec Eux pour les
instruire. Mais auant que de quitter le paÿs des
Ilinois il est bon que je rapporte ce que jay reconnu
de leurs Coustûmes et façons de faire.

SECTION 6ᴱᴹᴱ. DU NATUREL DES ILINOIS, DE LEURS
MŒURS & DE LEURS COUSTUMES, DE L'ESTIME
QU'ILS ONT POUR LE CALUMET OÙ PIPE A
PRENDRE DU TABAC, ET DE LA DANSE
QU'ILS FONT EN SON HONNEUR.

QUI dit Ilinois, c'est comme qui diroit en leur
langue, les hommes, Comme si les autres
Sauuages, aupres d'eux ne passoient que pour
des bestes, aussi faut-il aduoüer qu'ils ont un air
d'humanité que nous n'auons pas remarqué dans
les autres nations que nous auons veuës sur nostre
route. Le peu De séjour que jay fait parmy Eux ne
m'a pas permis de prendre toutes les Connoissances
que j'aurois souhaité; de toutes Leurs façons de
faire voicy ce que j'en ay remarqué.

Ils sont diuisés en plusieures bourgades dont quelqu'es vnes sont assés éloignées de celle dont nous

As they are of no great Value, we did not burden ourselves with Them.

We Slept in the Captain's Cabin, and on the following day we took Leave of him, promising to pass again by his village, within four moons. He Conducted us to our Canoes, with nearly 600 persons who witnessed our Embarkation, giving us every possible manifestation of the joy that Our visit had caused them. For my own part, I promised, on bidding them Adieu, that I would come the following year, and reside with Them to instruct them. But, before quitting the Ilinois country, it is proper that I should relate what I observed of their Customs and usages.

SECTION 6TH.   OF THE CHARACTER OF THE ILINOIS;
OF THEIR HABITS AND CUSTOMS; AND OF THE
ESTEEM THAT THEY HAVE FOR THE CALU-
MET, OR TOBACCO-PIPE, AND OF THE
DANCE THEY PERFORM IN ITS HONOR.

WHEN one speaks the word " Ilinois," it is as if one said in their language, " the men,"— As if the other Savages were looked upon by them merely as animals.[24] It must also be admitted that they have an air of humanity which we have not observed in the other nations that we have seen upon our route. The shortness Of my stay among Them did not allow me to secure all the Information that I would have desired; among all Their customs, the following is what I have observed.

They are divided into many villages, some of which are quite distant from that of which we speak, which is called peouarea. This causes some difference in their language, which, on the whole,

parlons qui s'appelle peoüarea, c'est ce qui met de la
difference en leur langue laquelle vniuersellement
tient de l'allegonquin de sorte que nous nous entendions facilement les vns les autres. Leur naturel
est doux et traitable, nous l'auons Experimenté dans
la reception qu'il nous ont faitte. Ils ont plusieurs
femmes donts ils sont Extremement jaloux, ils les
veillent auec vn grand soin et ils Leurs Couppent Le
néz ou les oreilles quand elles ne sont pas sages, j'en
ay veu plusieures qui portoient les marques de leurs
désordres. Ils ont le Corps bien fait, ils sont lestes
et fort adroits, a tirer de l'arc et de la flêche, Ils se
seruent aussi des fusils qu'ils acheptent des sauuages
nos alliés qui ont Commerce auec nos françois; Ils
en usent particulierement pour donner L épouuante
par le bruit et par la fumée a leurs Ennemys, qui
n'en n'ont point L usage, et n'en ont jamais veu
pour estre trop Éloigné vers le Couchant. Ils sont
belliqueux et se rendent redoutables aux peuples
Éloignés du sud et de L oüest où ils vont faire des
Esclaues, desquels ils se seruent pour trafiquer, les
vendant cherement a d'autres Nations, pour d'autres
Marchandises. Ces Sauuages si Eloignes chez qui
ils vont En guerre n'ont aucune Connoissance d'Europeans; ils ne scauent a que c'est ny de fer n'y de
Cuiure, et n'ont que des Cousteaux De pierre. quand
les Ilinois partent pour aller en guerre, il faut que
tout le bourg en soit aduertÿ par le grand Cry qu'ils
font a la porte de leurs Cabanes, le soir et Le Matin
auant que de partir. Les Capitaines se distinguent
des soldatz par des Escharpes rouges qu'ils portent,
elles sont faittes de Crin d'ours et du poil de bœufs
sauuages auec assés d'Industrie, ils se peignent le

resembles allegonquin, so that we easily understood
each other. They are of a gentle and tractable dis-
position; we Experienced this in the reception which
they gave us. They have several wives, of whom
they are Extremely jealous; they watch them very
closely, and Cut off Their noses or ears when they
misbehave. I saw several women who bore the
marks of their misconduct. Their Bodies are shapely; they are active and very skillful with bows and
arrows. They also use guns, which they buy from
our savage allies who Trade with our french. They
use them especially to inspire, through their noise
and smoke, terror in their Enemies; the latter do
not use guns, and have never seen any, since they
live too Far toward the West. They are warlike,
and make themselves dreaded by the Distant tribes
to the south and west, whither they go to procure
Slaves; these they barter, selling them at a high
price to other Nations, in exchange for other Wares.²⁵
Those very Distant Savages against whom they war
have no Knowledge of Europeans; neither do they
know anything of iron, or of Copper, and they have
only stone Knives. When the Ilinois depart to go
to war, the whole village must be notified by a loud
Shout, which is uttered at the doors of their Cabins,
the night and The Morning before their departure.
The Captains are distinguished from the warriors by
wearing red Scarfs. These are made, with considerable Skill, from the Hair of bears and wild cattle.
They paint their faces with red ocher, great quantities of which are found at a distance of some days'
journey from the village. They live by hunting,
game being plentiful in that country, and on indian
corn, of which they always have a good crop; conse-

visage d'un rouge de sanguine, dont il y a grande
quantité a quelques journées du bourg. ils viuent
de chasse, qui est abondante en ce paÿs et de bled
d'inde dont ils font tousjour une bonne recolte, aussi
n'ont-ils jamais souffert de famine, ils sement aussi
des febues et des melons qui sont Excellentz, surtout
ceux qui ont la graine rouge, leurs Citrouilles ne sont
pas des meillieures, ils les font secher au secher au
soleil pour les manger pendant L'hyuer et le primp-
temps,   Leurs Cabanes sont fort grandes, elles sont
Couuertes et pauées de nattes faittes de Joncs; Ils
trouuent toutes Leurs vaisselle dans le bois et Leurs
Cuilliers dans la teste des bœufs dontz ils sçauent si
bien accommoder le Crane qu'ils s'en seruent pour
manger aisement leur sagamité.

Ils sont liberaux dans leurs maladies, et Croÿent
que les medicamens qu'on leurs donne, operent a
proportion des presens qu'ils auront fais au medicin.
Ils n'ont que des peaux pour habitz, les femmes sont
tousjours vestuës fort modestement et dans une
grande bien seance, au lieu que les hommes ne se
mettent pas en peine de se Couurir.   Je ne scais par
quelle superstition quelques Ilinois, aussi bien que
quelques Nadoüessi, estant encor jeunes prennent
l'habit des femmes qu'ils gardent toute leur vie.   Il
y a du mystere; Car ils ne se marient jamais, et font
gloire de s'abbaisser a faire tout ce que font les
femmes; ils vont pourtant en guerre, mais ils ne
peuuent se seruir que de la massuë, et non pas de
l'arc n'y de la flêche qui sont les armes propres des
hommes, ils assistent a toutes les jongleriës et aux
danses solemnelles qui se font a l'honneur du Calumet, ils y chantent mais ils n'y peuuent pas danser,

quently, they have never suffered from famine.
They also sow beans and melons, which are Excellent, especially those that have red seeds. Their
Squashes are not of the best; they dry them in the
sun, to eat them during The winter and the spring.
Their Cabins are very large, and are Roofed and
floored with mats made of Rushes. They make all
Their utensils of wood, and Their Ladles out of the
heads of cattle, whose Skulls they know so well how
to prepare that they use these ladles with ease for
eating their sagamité.

They are liberal in cases of illness, and Think that
the effect of the medicines administered to them is in
proportion to the presents given to the physician.
Their garments consist only of skins; the women
are always clad very modestly and very becomingly,
while the men do not take the trouble to Cover themselves. I know not through what superstition some
Ilinois, as well as some Nadouessi, while still young,
assume the garb of women, and retain it throughout
their lives. There is some mystery in this, For they
never marry and glory in demeaning themselves to
do everything that the women do. They go to war,
however, but can use only clubs, and not bows and
arrows, which are the weapons proper to men. They
are present at all the juggleries, and at the solemn
dances in honor of the Calumet; at these they sing,
but must not dance. They are summoned to the
Councils, and nothing can be decided without their
advice. Finally, through their profession of leading
an Extraordinary life, they pass for Manitous,— That
is to say, for Spirits,— or persons of Consequence.[26]

There remains no more, except to speak of the
Calumet. There is nothing more mysterious or more

ils sont appellés aux Conseils, ou l'on ne peut rien
decider sans leurs aduis; Enfin par la profession
quils font d'une vie Extresordinaire, ils passent pour
des Manitous C'est a dire pour des Genies ou des
personnes de Consequence.

Il ne reste plus qu'a parler du Calumet, il n'est
rien parmy eux ny de plus mysterieux n'y de plus
recommandable, on ne rend pas tant d honneur aux
Couronnes et aux sceptres des Roÿs qu'ils luy en
rendent; il semble estre le Dieu de la paix et de la
guerre, l'Arbitre de la vie et de la mort.   C'est assez
de le porter sur soy et de le faire voir pour marcher
en assurance au milieu des Ennemÿs, qui dans le fort
du Combat mettent bas Les armes quand on le montre.
C'est pour Cela que les Ilinois m'en donnerent un
pour me seruir de sauuegarde parmy toutes les
Nations par lesquelles je deuois passer dans mon voÿage.   il y a un Calumet pour La paix et un pour la
guerre, qui ne sont distingués que par la Couleur des
plumages dontz ils sont ornés: Le Rouge est marque
de guerre, ils s'en seruent encor pour terminer Leur
differents, pour affermir Leurs alliances et pour
parler aux Estrangers.   Il est composé d'une pierre
rouge polie comme du marbre et percée d'une telle
façon qu'un bout sert à recevoir le tabac et l'autre
s'enclave dans le manche, qui est un baston de deux
pieds de long, gros comme une canne ordinaire et
percé par le milieu; il est embelly de la teste et du
col de divers oiseaux, dont le plumage est tres beau;
ils y ajoutent aussi de grandes plumes rouges, vertes
et d'autres couleurs, dont il est tout empanaché;
ils en font estat particulièrement, parcequ'ils le re-
gardent comme le calumet du Soleil; et de fait, ils le

respected among them. Less honor is paid to the
Crowns and scepters of Kings than the Savages
bestow upon this. It seems to be the God of peace
and of war, the Arbiter of life and of death. It has
but to be carried upon one's person, and displayed,
to enable one to walk safely through the midst of
Enemies — who, in the hottest of the Fight, lay
down Their arms when it is shown. For That reason, the Ilinois gave me one, to serve as a safeguard
among all the Nations through whom I had to pass
during my voyage. There is a Calumet for peace,
and one for war, which are distinguished solely by
the Color of the feathers with which they are adorned;
Red is a sign of war. They also use it to put an end
to Their disputes, to strengthen Their alliances, and
to speak to Strangers.[27] It is fashioned from a red
stone, polished like marble, and bored in such a
manner that one end serves as a receptacle for the
tobacco, while the other fits into the stem; this is a
stick two feet long, as thick as an ordinary cane, and
bored through the middle. It is ornamented with
the heads and necks of various birds, whose plumage
is very beautiful. To these they also add large feathers,— red, green, and other colors,— wherewith the
whole is adorned. They have a great regard for it,
because they look upon it as the calumet of the Sun;
and, in fact, they offer it to the latter to smoke when
they wish to obtain a calm, or rain, or fine weather.
They scruple to bathe themselves at the beginning
of Summer, or to eat fresh fruit, until after they
have performed the dance, which they do as follows:

The Calumet dance, which is very famous among
these peoples, is performed solely for important reasons; sometimes to strengthen peace, or to unite

luy presentent pour fumer quand ils veulent obtenir
du calme, ou de la pluye, ou du beau temps. Ils
font scrupule de se baigner au commencement de
l'Esté, ou de manger des fruits nouveaux qu'après
l'avoir dancé. En voicy la façon.

La dance du Calumet, qui est fort celebre parmi
ces peuples, ne se fait que pour des sujets conside-
rables; quelquefois c'est pour affermir la paix, ou se
reünir pour quelque grande guerre; c'est d'autres
fois pour une réjouissance publique, tantost on en
fait honneur à une Nation qu'on invite d'y assister,
tantost ils s'en servent à la reception de quelque personne considerable, comme s'ils vouloient luy donner
le divertissement du Bal ou de la Comedie; l'Hyver
la ceremonie se fait dans une Cabane, l'Esté c'est en
raze campagne. La place étant choisie, on l'envi-
ronne tout à l'entour d'arbres pour metre tout le
monde à l'ombre de leurs feüillages, pour se défendre
des chaleurs du Soleil; on étend une grande natte
de joncs peinte de diverses couleurs au milieu de la
place; elle sert comme de tapis pour mettre dessus
avec honneur le Dieu de celuy qui fait la Dance; car
chacun a le sien, qu'ils appellent leur Manitou, c'est
un serpent ou un oyseau ou chose semblable, qu'ils
ont resvé en dormant et en qui ils mettent toute leur
confiance pour le succez de leur guerre, de leur pesche
et de leur chasse: près de ce Manitou, et à sa droite,
on met le Calumet en l'honneur de qui se fait la feste
et tout à l'entour on fait comme une trophée et on
étend les armes dont se servent les guerriers de ces
Nations, sçavoir la massüe, la hache d'arme, l'arc, le
carquois et les fleches.

Les choses estant ainsi disposées et l'heure de la
Dance approchant, ceux qui sont nommez pour chan-

themselves for some great war; at other times, for
public rejoicing. Sometimes they thus do honor to
a Nation who are invited to be present; sometimes
it is danced at the reception of some important per-
sonage, as if they wished to give him the diversion
of a Ball or a Comedy. In Winter, the ceremony
takes place in a Cabin; in Summer, in the open
fields. When the spot is selected, it is completely
surrounded by trees, so that all may sit in the shade
afforded by their leaves, in order to be protected
from the heat of the Sun. A large mat of rushes,
painted in various colors, is spread in the middle of
the place, and serves as a carpet upon which to place
with honor the God of the person who gives the
Dance; for each has his own god, which they call
their Manitou. This is a serpent, a bird, or other
similar thing, of which they have dreamed while
sleeping, and in which they place all their confidence
for the success of their war, their fishing, and their
hunting. Near this Manitou, and at its right, is
placed the Calumet in honor of which the feast is
given; and all around it a sort of trophy is made,
and the weapons used by the warriors of those
Nations are spread, namely: clubs, war-hatchets,
bows, quivers, and arrows.

Everything being thus arranged, and the hour of
the Dance drawing near, those who have been appointed to sing take the most honorable place under
the branches; these are the men and women who
are gifted with the best voices, and who sing together
in perfect harmony. Afterward, all come to take
their seats in a circle under the branches; but each
one, on arriving, must salute the Manitou. This he
does by inhaling the smoke, and blowing it from his

ter prennent la place la plus honorable sous les feüillages: ce sont les hommes et les femmes qui ont les
plus belles voix, et qui s'accordent parfaitement bien
ensemble, tout le monde vient en suite se placer en
rond sous les branches, mais chacun en arrivant doit
salüer le Manitou, ce qu'il fait en petunant et jettant
de sa bouche la fumée sur luy comme s'il luy presentoit de l'encens; chacun va d'abord avec respect
prendre le Calumet et le soutenant des deux mains,
il le fait dancer en cadence, s'accordant bien avec
l'air des chansons; il luy fait faire des figures bien
differentes, tantost il le fait voir à toute l'assemblée
se [le — *Martin*] tournant de coté et d'autre; après
cela, celuy qui doit commencer la Danse paroist au
milieu de l'assemblée, et va d'abord, et tantost il le
presente au soleil, comme s'il le voulait faire fumer,
tantost il l'incline vers la terre, d'autres fois [et
tantôt — *Martin*] il luy étend les aisles comme pour
voler, d'autres fois il l'approche de la bouche des
assistans, afin qu'ils fument, le tout en cadence; et
c'est comme la premiere Scene du Ballet.

La seconde consiste en un Combat qui se fait au
son d'une espece de tambour, qui succede au chansons, ou mesme qui s'y joignant, s'accordent fort
bien ensemble: le Danseur fait signe à quelque guer-
rier de venir prendre les armes qui sont sur la natte
et l'invite a se battre au son des tambours: celuy-cy
s'approche, prend l'arc et la fléche, avec la hache
d'armes et commence le duël contre l'autre, qui n'a
point d'autre défense que le Calumet. Ce spectacle
est fort agreable, sur tout le faisant toûjours en
cadence; car l'un attaque, l'autre se deffend; l'un
porte des coups, l'autre les pare; l'un fuit, l'autre le
poursuit et puis celuy qui fuyoit tourne visage et

mouth upon the Manitou, as if he were offering to
it incense. Every one, at the outset, takes the Calumet in a respectful manner, and, supporting it with
both hands, causes it to dance in cadence, keeping
good time with the air of the songs. He makes it
execute many differing figures; sometimes he shows
it to the whole assembly, turning himself from one
side to the other. After that, he who is to begin
the Dance appears in the middle of the assembly,
and at once continues this.[28] Sometimes he offers
it to the sun, as if he wished the latter to smoke it;
sometimes he inclines it toward the earth; again, he
makes it spread its wings, as if about to fly; at other
times, he puts it near the mouths of those present,
that they may smoke. The whole is done in
cadence; and this is, as it were, the first Scene of
the Ballet.

The second consists of a Combat carried on to the
sound of a kind of drum, which succeeds the songs,
or even unites with them, harmonizing very well
together. The Dancer makes a sign to some
warrior to come to take the arms which lie upon
the mat, and invites him to fight to the sound of
the drums. The latter approaches, takes up the bow
and arrows, and the war-hatchet, and begins the
duel with the other, whose sole defense is the Calumet. This spectacle is very pleasing, especially as
all is done in cadence; for one attacks, the other
defends himself; one strikes blows, the other parries
them; one takes to flight, the other pursues; and
then he who was fleeing faces about, and causes his
adversary to flee. This is done so well — with slow
and measured steps, and to the rhythmic sound of the
voices and drums — that it might pass for a very fine

fait fuïr son ennemy; ce qui se passe si bien par
mesure et à pas comptez et au son réglé des voix et
des tambours, que cela pourrait passer pour une
assez belle entrée de Ballet en France. La troisieme
Scene consiste en un grand Discours que fait celuy
qui tient le Calumet, car le Combat estant fini sans
sang répandu, il raconte les batailles où il s'est trou-
vé, les victoires qu'il a remportées; il nomme les
Nations, les lieux et les Captifs qu'il a fait; et pour
recompense celuy qui préside à la Danse luy fait
present d'une belle robe de Castor, ou de quelqu'autre
chose et l'ayant receu il va presenter le Calumet à
un autre, celui-ci à un troisiéme, et ainsi de tous les
autres, jusques à ce que tous ayant fait leur devoir, le
President fait present du Calumet mesme à la Nation
qui a esté invitée à cette Ceremonie, pour marque
de la paix eternelle qui sera entre les deux peuples.

Voicy quelqu'une des Chansons qu'ils ont coûtume
de chanter, ils leur donnent un certain tour [ton —
Martin] qu'on ne peut assez exprimer par la Notte,
qui neanmoins en fait tout la grace.

Ninahani, ninahani ninahani nani ongo.

SECTION 7ᴱᴹᴱ. DEPART DU PERE DES ILINOIS: DES
MONSTRES EN PEINTURE QU'IL A VEU SUR LA
GRANDE RIUIERE MISSISIPI: DE LA RIUIERE
PEKITANOUÏ. CONTINUATION DU VOŸAGE.

NOUS prenons congé de nos Ilinois sur la fin de
Juin, vers les trois heures apres midy, nous
nous embarquons à la veuë de tous ces peuples,
qui admiroient nos petits Canots, n'en ayant jamais
veu de semblables.

Nous descendons suivant le courant de la rivière
appelle Pekitanoüi, qui se décharge dans Mississipy

opening of a Ballet in France. The third Scene consists of a lofty Discourse, delivered by him who
holds the Calumet; for, when the Combat is ended
without bloodshed, he recounts the battles at which
he has been present, the victories that he has won,
the names of the Nations, the places, and the Captives whom he has made. And, to reward him, he
who presides at the Dance makes him a present of a
fine robe of Beaver-skins, or some other article.
Then, having received it, he hands the Calumet to
another, the latter to a third, and so on with all the
others, until every one has done his duty; then the
President presents the Calumet itself to the Nation
that has been invited to the Ceremony, as a token of
the everlasting peace that is to exist between the
two peoples.

Here is one of the Songs that they are in the habit
of singing. They give it a certain turn which
cannot be sufficiently expressed by Note, but which
nevertheless constitutes all its grace.

Ninahani, ninahani, ninahani, nani ongo.[29]

SECTION 7TH. DEPARTURE OF THE FATHER FROM THE
ILINOIS; OF THE PAINTED MONSTERS WHICH HE SAW
UPON THE GREAT RIVER MISSISIPI; OF THE RIVER
PEKITANOUÏ. CONTINUATION OF THE VOYAGE.[30]

WE take leave of our Ilinois at the end of June,
about three o'clock in the afternoon. We
embark in the sight of all the people, who admire
our little Canoes, for they have never seen any like
them.

We descend, following the current of the river
called Pekitanoui, which discharges into the Mississipy, flowing from the Northwest. I shall have

venant du Nord-Oüest de la quelle j'ay quelque chose
de considerable à dire, apres que j'auray raconté ce
que j'ay remarqué sur cette riviere.

passant proche des rochers assez hautz qui bordent
la riuiere, J'apperceu un simple qui m'a paru fort
Extraordinair. La racine est semblable a des petitz
naueaux attachez les uns aux autres par les petitz
filetz qui ont le gout de carote; de cette racine sort vne
feuille large Comme la main espaisses d'un demy doigt
auec des taches au milieu, de cette feuille, naissent
d'autres feuilles semblables aux plaques qui seruent
de flambeaux dans nos sales, et chasque feuille porte
Cinq ou six fleurs jaunes en forme de Clochettes.

Nous trouuâmes quantité de meures aussi grosses
que Celle de france, et un petit fruict que nous
prismes d'abord pour des oliues, mais il auoit le gout
d'orange, et un aultre fruit gros Comme vn œuf de
poule, nous le fendismes en deux, et parurent deux
separations, dans chasqu'une desquelles il y a 8 ou 10
fruitz enchassés, ils ont la figure d'amande et sont
fort bons quand ils sont meurs; L'arbre neamoins
qui les porte a tres mauuaise odeur, et sa feuille ressemble a Celle de noÿer, il se trouue aussi dans Les
prairies un fruit semblable a des Noisettes mais plus
tendre; Les feuilles sont fort grandes, et viennent
d'une tige au bout de laquelle est une teste semblable a Celle d'un tournesol, dans laquelle toutes
ses Noisettes sont proprement arrangées, elle sont
fort bonnes et Cuites et Crües.

Comme nous Cottoions des roches affreux pour
Leur haulteur et pour leur Longour; Nous vismes
sur un de ces roches deux monstres en peinture qui
Nous firent peur d'abord et sur Lesquels les sauuages
les plus hardys n'osent pas arrester Longtemps les

something important to say about it, when I shall
have related all that I observed along this river.[31]

While passing near the rather high rocks that line
the river, I noticed a simple which seemed to me
very Extraordinary. The root is like small turnips
fastened together by little filaments, which taste like
carrots. From this root springs a leaf as wide As
one's hand, and half a finger thick, with spots.
From the middle of this leaf spring other leaves,
resembling the sconces used for candles in our halls;
and each leaf bears Five or six yellow flowers shaped
like little Bells.

We found quantities of mulberries, as large as
Those of france; and a small fruit which we at first
took for olives, but which tasted like oranges; and
another fruit as large As a hen's egg. We cut it in
halves, and two divisions appeared, in each of which
8 to 10 fruits were encased; these are shaped like
almonds, and are very good when ripe. Nevertheless, The tree that bears them has a very bad odor,
and its leaves resemble Those of the walnut-tree.
In These prairies there is also a fruit similar to
Hazelnuts, but more delicate; The leaves are very
large, and grow from a stalk at the end of which is
a head similar to That of a sunflower, in which all
its Nuts are regularly arranged. These are very
good, both Cooked and Raw.[32]

While Skirting some rocks, which by Their height
and Length inspired awe, We saw upon one of them
two painted monsters which at first made Us afraid,
and upon Which the boldest savages dare not Long
rest their eyes. They are as large As a calf; they
have Horns on their heads Like those of deer, a
horrible look, red eyes, a beard Like a tiger's, a face

yeux; ils sont gros Comme vn veau. ils ont des Cornes en teste Comme des cheureils; un regard affreux, des yeux rouges, une barbe Comme d'un tygre, la face a quelque chose de l'homme, le corps Couuert d'écailles, et La queuë si Longue qu'elle fait tout le tour du Corps passant par dessus la teste et retournant entre les jambes elle se termine en queuë de Poisson. Le vert, Le rouge et Le noirastre sont les trois Couleurs qui Le Composent: au reste ces 2 monstres sont si bien peint que nous ne pouuons pas croire qu'aucun sauuage en soit L'autheur, puisque Les bons peintres en france auroient peine a si bien faire, veuque d'ailleurs ils sont si hauts sur le rocher qu'il est difficile d'y atteindre Commodément pour les peindre. voicy a peu pres La figure de ces monstres Comme nous L'auons Contretirée.

Comme nous entretenions sur ces monstres, voguant paisiblement dans vne belle Eau claire et dormante nous entredisme le bruit d'un rapide, dans lequel nous allions tomber. Je n'ay rien veu de plus affreux, vn ambaras de gros arbres entiers, de branches, & islets flotans, sortoit de L embouchure de La riuiere pekistanouï auec tant d'impetuosité qu'on ne pouuoit s'exposer a passer au trauers sans grand danger. L'agitation estoit telle que l'eau en estoit toute boueuse et ne pouuoit s'epurer.

Pekitanouï est une riuiere Considerable qui venant d'assez Loing du Costé du Noroüest, se décharge dans Missisipi, plusieures Bourgades de sauuages sont placées le long de cette riuiere, et j espere par son moyen faire la découuerte de la mer vermeille ou de Californie.

Nous jugeons bien par Le Rund de vent que tient Missisipï, si elle Continuë dans la mesme route,

somewhat like a man's, a body Covered with scales, and so Long A tail that it winds all around the Body, passing above the head and going back between the legs, ending in a Fish's tail. Green, red, and black are the three Colors composing the Picture. More-over, these 2 monsters are so well painted that we cannot believe that any savage is their author; for good painters in france would find it difficult to paint so well,—and, besides, they are so high up on the rock that it is difficult to reach that place Conven-iently to paint them. Here is approximately The shape of these monsters, As we have faithfully Copied It.[38]

While conversing about these monsters, sailing quietly in clear and calm Water, we heard the noise of a rapid, into which we were about to run. I have seen nothing more dreadful. An accumulation of large and entire trees, branches, and floating islands, was issuing from The mouth of The river pekistanouï, with such impetuosity that we could not without great danger risk passing through it. So great was the agitation that the water was very muddy, and could not become clear.

Pekitanouï is a river of Considerable size, coming from the Northwest, from a great Distance; and it discharges into the Missisipi. There are many Vil-lages of savages along this river, and I hope by its means to discover the vermillion or California sea.

Judging from The Direction of the course of the Missisipï, if it Continue the same way, we think that it discharges into the mexican gulf. It would be a great advantage to find the river Leading to the southern sea, toward California; and, As I have said, this is what I hope to do by means of the Pekitanouï,

qu'elle a sa décharge dans le golphe mexique; il
seroit bien aduantageux de trouuer celle qui Conduit
a la mer du sud, vers la Californie, et c'est Comme
j'ay dit ce que j'espere de rencontrer par Peᴋitanouï
suiuant le rapport que m'en ont fait les sauuages,
desquels, jay appris qu'en refoullant cette riuiere
pendant 5 ou 6 Journées on trouue vne belle prairie
de 20 ou 30 Lieuës de Long, il faut la trauerser allant
au Noroüest, elle se termine a vne autre petite
riuiere, sur laquelle on peut s'embarquer, n'étant
pas bien difficile de transporter les Canotz par vn si
beau paÿs tel qu'est cette prairie.   Cette 2de. Riuiere
a son Cours vers Le suroüest pendant 10 ou 15 Lieuës
apres quoy elle entre dans un petit Lac *profond* [qui
est la source d'une autre rivière profonde,— *substituted
by Dablon*], laquelle va au Couchant, où elle se jette
dans La mer.   je ne doubte presque point que ce ne
soit La mer vermeille, et je ne desespere pas d'en faire
un jour La découuerte, si Dieu m'en fait la grace et me
donne La santé affin de pouuoir publier L'Euangile a
tous Les peuples de ce nouueau monde, qui ont Croupi
si Longtemps dans les tenebres de L'infidelité.

Reprenons nostre Route apres nous estre Eschapés
Comme Nous auons pû de ce dangereux rapide Causé
par L'ambaras dont jay parlé.

SECTION 8EME.   DES NOUVEAU PAYS QUE LE PERE DÉ-
COUVRE:—DIVERSES PARTICULARITÉS-—RENCONTRE
DE QUELQUES SAUVAGES; PREMIERES NOUVELLES
DE LA MER ET DES EUROPEANS.   GRAND DAN-
GER EVITÉ PAR LE MOYEN DU CALUMET.

A PRES avoir fait environ 20 Lieües droit au sud et
un peu moins au sudest nous nous trouvons a
une riviere nommée ouaboukigou dont L embouchure

according to the reports made to me by the savages.
From them I have learned that, by ascending this
river for 5 or 6 Days, one reaches a fine prairie, 20
or 30 Leagues Long. This must be crossed in a
Northwesterly direction, and it terminates at another
small river,—on which one may embark, for it is
not very difficult to transport Canoes through so fine
a country as that prairie. This 2nd River Flows
toward The southwest for 10 or 15 Leagues, after
which it enters a Lake, small and deep [the source
of another deep river—*substituted by Dablon*], which
flows toward the West, where it falls into The sea.[34]
I have hardly any doubt that it is The vermillion
sea, and I do not despair of discovering It some day,
if God grant me the grace and The health to do so,
in order that I may preach The Gospel to all The
peoples of this new world who have so Long
Groveled in the darkness of infidelity.

Let us resume our Route, after Escaping As best
We could from the dangerous rapid Caused by The
obstruction which I have mentioned.

SECTION 8TH.   OF THE NEW COUNTRIES DISCOVERED
BY THE FATHER.   VARIOUS PARTICULARS.   MEET-
ING WITH SOME SAVAGES.   FIRST NEWS OF THE
SEA AND OF EUROPEANS.   GREAT DANGER
AVOIDED BY MEANS OF THE CALUMET.

AFTER proceeding about 20 Leagues straight to the
south, and a little less to the southeast, we
found ourselves at a river called ouaboukigou, The
mouth of which is at the 36th degree of latitude.
Before reaching it, we passed by a Place that is
dreaded by the Savages, because they believe that a
manitou is there,—that is to say, a demon,—that

est par les 36 degrez d'elevation. Avant que d'y
arriver nous passons par un Lieu redoutable aux Sauvages parcequ'ils estiment qu'il y a un manitou c'est
a dire un demon qui devore Les passans, et c'est
dequoy nous menaçoient Les sauvages qui nous
vouloient détourner de nostre entreprise. voicy ce
demon, c'est une petite anse de rochers haulte de 20
pieds ou se dégorge tout Le Courant de la riviere
Lequel estant repoussé contre celuy qui Le suit et
arresté par une Isle qui est proche, est Contraint de
passer par un petit Canal, ce qui ne se fait pas sans un
furieux Combat de toutes ces eaux qui rebroussent
Les unes sur Les autres et sans un grand tintamarre
qui donne de la terreur a des sauvages qui craignent
tout.   mais cela ne nous empéche point de passer et
d'arriver a ȣabȣkigȣ. Cette riviere vient des terres
du Levant où sont les peuples qu'on appelle Chaouanons, en si grand nombre qu'en un quartier on
Compte jusqua 23 villages et 15 en un aultre assez
proches Les uns des aultres; ils ne sont nullement
guerriers, et ce sont les peuples que les Iroquois vont
chercher si loing pour Leur faire la guerre sans
aucun sujet, et parceque ces pauvres gens ne scavent
pas se deffendre, ils se laissent prendre et emmener
Comme des trouppeaux, et tout innocents qu'ils sont,
ils ne laissent pas de ressentir quelque fois La
barbarie des Iroquois qui Les bruslent cruellement.
    Un peu au dessus de cette riviere dont ie viens de
parler sont des falaises ou nos francois ont appercue
une mine de fer qu'ils jugent tres abondante, il y en
a plusieures veines et un lit d'un pied de hauteur;
on en voit de gros morceaux liez avec des Cailloux.
Il s'y trouve d'une terre grasse de trois sortes de

devours travelers; and The savages, who wished to
divert us from our undertaking, warned us against
it.   This is the demon: there is a small cove, surrounded by rocks 20 feet high, into which The whole
Current of the river rushes; and, being pushed back
against the waters following It, and checked by an
Island near by, the Current is Compelled to pass
through a narrow Channel.   This is not done without a violent Struggle between all these waters,
which force one another back, or without a great din,
which inspires terror in the savages, who fear everything.   But this did not prevent us from passing,
and arriving at Waboukigou.[35]   This river flows
from the lands of the East, where dwell the people
called Chaouanons in so great numbers that in one
district there are as many as 23 villages, and 15 in
another, quite near one another.   They are not at
all warlike, and are the nations whom the Iroquois
go so far to seek, and war against without any reason; and, because these poor people cannot defend
themselves, they allow themselves to be captured
and taken Like flocks of sheep; and, innocent though
they are, they nevertheless sometimes experience
The barbarity of the Iroquois, who cruelly burn
Them.[36]

A short distance above the river of which I have
just spoken are cliffs, on which our frenchmen noticed
an iron mine, which they consider very rich.   There
are several veins of ore, and a bed a foot thick, and
one sees large masses of it united with Pebbles.   A
sticky earth is found there, of three different colors —
purple, violet, and Red.   The water in which the
latter is washed assumes a bloody tinge.   There is
also very heavy, red sand.   I placed some on a

couleurs, de pourpre, de violet, et des Rouges.
L'eau dans laquelle on la lave prend la couleur de
sang. Il y a aussi d'un sable rouge fort pesant.
J'en mis sur un aviron qui en prit la couleur si fortement, que L'eau ne la pût effacer pendant 15 jours
que je m'en servois pour nager.

C'est icy que nous Commencons a voir des Cannes
ou gros roseaux qui sont sur le bord de la riviere,
elles ont un vert fort agreable, tous les nœuds sont
couronnez de feüilles Longues, estroittes et pointües,
elles sont fort hautes et en si grande quantité que
Les bœufs sauvages ont peine de les forcer.

Jusqua present nous n'avions point estez incom-
modés Les maringouins, mais nous entrons comme
dans leur pays. Voicy ce que font les sauvages de
ces quartiers pour s'en deffendre; ils elevent un
eschaffault dont le plancher n'est fait que de perches,
et par consequent est percé a jour affinque la fumée
du feu qu'ils font dessous passe au travers et chasse
ces petitz animaux qui ne la peuvent supporter, on
se couche sur les perches au dessus desquelles sont
des escorces estendües contre la pluye. Cet eschaffault leur sert encor contre Les chaleurs excessives
et Insupportables de ce pays, car on s'y met a
l'ombre a l'estage d'en bas, et on si garantit des rayons du soleil, prenant le frais du vent qui passe
librement autravers de cet eschaffault

Dans le mesme dessein nous fusmes contraincts de
faire sur L'eau une espace de cabane avec nos voiles
pour nous mettre a couvert et des maringouins et des
rayons du soleil, comme nous nous laissions aller en
cet estat au gré de L'eau, nous apperceumes a terre
des sauvages armez de fusils avec lesquels ils nous

paddle, which was dyed with its color — so deeply
that The water could not wash it away during the
15 days while I used it for paddling.

Here we Began to see Canes, or large reeds, which
grow on the bank of the river; their color is a very
pleasing green; all the nodes are marked by a Crown
of Long, narrow, and pointed leaves. They are very
high, and grow so thickly that The wild cattle have
some difficulty in forcing their way through them.

Hitherto, we had not suffered any inconvenience
from mosquitoes; but we were entering into their
home, as it were. This is what the savages of this
quarter do to protect themselves against them. They
erect a scaffolding, the floor of which consists only
of poles, so that it is open to the air in order that
the smoke of the fire made underneath may pass
through, and drive away those little creatures, which
cannot endure it; the savages lie down upon the
poles, over which bark is spread to keep off rain.
These scaffoldings also serve them as protection
against The excessive and Unbearable heat of this
country; for they lie in the shade, on the floor
below, and thus protect themselves against the sun's
rays, enjoying the cool breeze that circulates freely
through the scaffolding.

With the same object, we were compelled to erect
a sort of cabin on The water, with our sails as a protection against the mosquitoes and the rays of the
sun. While drifting down with The current, in this
condition, we perceived on land some savages armed
with guns, who awaited us. I at once offered them
my plumed calumet, while our frenchmen prepared
for defense, but delayed firing, that The savages
might be the first to discharge their guns. I spoke

attendoient; Je leur presentay d'abord mon calumet
empanaché pendant que nos francois se mettent en
deffense, et attendoient a tirer, que Les sauvages
eussent fait la premiere décharge; je leur parlay en
huron, mais ils me repondirent par un mot qui me
sembloit nous declarer la guerre, ils avoient neanmoins autant de peur que nous, et ceque nous
prenions pour signal de guerre, estoit une Invitation
qu'ils nous faisoit de nous approcher, pour nous
donner a manger; Nous debarquons donc et nous
entrons dans leur Cabanes où ils nous presente du
bœuf sauvage et de l'huile d'ours, avec des prunes
blanches qui sont tres excellentes.   Ils ont des fusils,
des haches, des houës, des Cousteaux de La rassade,
des bouteilles de verre double ou ils mettent Leur
poudre, ils ont Les cheveux longs, et se marquent
par le corps a la façon des hiroquois; les femmes
sont coiffées et vestuës a la façon des huronnes, ils
nous assurerent qu'ils n'y avoient plus que dix jour-
nees jusqua La mer, qu'ils acheptoient Les estoffes
et toutes autres marchandise des Europeans qui
estoient du coste de L'est, que ces Europeans avoient
des chapeletz, et des images, qu'ils jouoient des
Instrumentz, qu'il y en avoit qui estoient faitz Comme
moy, et qu'ils en estoient bien recue; Cependant
je ne vis personne qui me parut avoir recue aucune
instruction pour la foy, je Leurs en donnay ceque je
pûs avec quelques medailles.

Ces nouvelles animerent nos courages et nous firent
prendre L'aviron avec une Nouvelle ardeur.   Nous
avançons donc, et nous ne voions plus tant de prairies, parceque les 2 costéz de La riviere sont bordéz
de hauts bois.   Les cottonniers, Les ormes, et les

to them in huron, but they answered me by a word
which seemed to me a declaration of war against us.
However, they were as frightened as we were; and
what we took for a signal for battle was an Invitation that they gave us to draw near, that they might
give us food. We therefore landed, and entered their
Cabins, where they offered us meat from wild cattle
and bear's grease, with white plums, which are very
good. They have guns, hatchets, hoes, Knives,
beads, and flasks of double glass, in which they put
Their powder. They wear Their hair long, and
tattoo their bodies after the hiroquois fashion. The
women wear head-dresses and garments like those of
the huron women. They assured us that we were
no more than ten days' journey from The sea; that
they bought cloth and all other goods from the
Europeans who lived to The east, that these Europeans had rosaries and pictures; that they played
upon Instruments; that some of them looked Like
me, and had been received by these savages kindly.
Nevertheless, I saw none who seemed to have
received any instruction in the faith; I gave Them
as much as I could, with some medals.[37]

This news animated our courage, and made us
paddle with Fresh ardor. We thus push forward,
and no longer see so many prairies, because both
shores of The river are bordered with lofty trees.
The cottonwood, elm, and basswood trees there are
admirable for Their height and thickness. The
great numbers of wild cattle, which we heard bel-
lowing, lead us to believe that The prairies are near.
We also saw Quail on the water's edge. We killed
a little parroquet, one half of whose head was red,
The other half and The Neck yellow, and The whole

bois blancs y sont admirables pour Leur haulteur, et
Leur grosseur. La grande quantité de bœufs sauvages que nous entendions meugler nous fait croire
que Les prairies sont proches: Nous voions aussi des
Cailles sur l'aborde de L'eau; nous avons tué un
petit perroquet qui avoit la moitié de la teste rouge,
L'autre et Le Col jaune, et tout Le corps vert.
Nous estions descendus proche des 33 degrez d'es-
levation ayant presque tousjours esté Vers Le sud,
quand nous apperceûmes un village sur Le bord de
L'eau nommé Mitchigamea; Nous eumes recours a
nostre Patrone et a nostre conductrice La Sᵗᵉ VIERGE
IMMACULÉE, et nous avions bien besoin de son assistance, Car nous entendisme de loing Les sauvages
qui s'animoient au Combat par leurs crys Continuels;
ils estoient armes d'arcs, de flêches, de haches, de
massües, et de boucliers; ils se mirent en estat de
nous attaquer par terre, et par eau; un partie s'embarque dans de grand canotz de bois, les uns pour
monter la riviere; Les autres pour la descendre, affin
de nous Coupper chemin, et nous envelopper de tous
costez; Ceux qui estoient a terre alloient et venoient
comme pour commencer L'attaque; De fait de
Jeunes hommes se jetterent a L'eau, pour se venir
saisir de mon Canot, mais le courant Les ayant contraint de reprendre terre, un deux nous jetta sa
massüe qui passa par dessus nous sans nous frapper;
J'avois beau montrer Le calumet, et leur faire signe
par gestes que nous ne venions pas en guerre; L'a-
larme continuoit tousjour et l'on se preparoit deia a
nous percer de flêches de toutes parts quand Dieu
toucha soûdainment le cœur des viellards qui
estoient sur la bord de l'eau sans doubte par la veüe

body green. We had gone down to near the 33rd degree of latitude having proceeded nearly all the time in a southerly direction, when we perceived a village on The water's edge called Mitchigamea.[38] We had recourse to our Patroness and guide, The Blessed VIRGIN IMMACULATE; and we greatly needed her assistance, For we heard from afar The savages who were inciting one another to the Fray by their Continual yells. They were armed with bows, arrows, hatchets, clubs, and shields. They prepared to attack us, on both land and water; part of them embarked in great wooden canoes—some to ascend, others to descend the river, in order to Intercept us and surround us on all sides. Those who were on land came and went, as if to commence The attack. In fact, some Young men threw themselves into The water, to come and seize my Canoe; but the current compelled Them to return to land. One of them then hurled his club, which passed over without striking us. In vain I showed The calumet, and made them signs that we were not coming to war against them. The alarm continued, and they were already preparing to pierce us with arrows from all sides, when God suddenly touched the hearts of the old men, who were standing at the water's edge. This no doubt happened through the sight of our Calumet, which they had not clearly distinguished from afar; but as I did not cease displaying it, they were influenced by it, and checked the ardor of their Young men. Two of these elders even,—after casting into our canoe, as if at our feet, Their bows and quivers, to reassure us—entered the canoe, and made us approach the shore, whereon we landed, not without fear on our part. At first, we had to

de nostre Calumet qu'ils n'avoient pas bien reconnu
de loing, mais comme je ne cessois de le faire
paroistre, ils en furent touchez arresterent l'ardeur
de leur Jeunesse, et mesme deux de ces anciens ayant
jettez dans nostre canot comme a nos pieds Leurs
arcs et Leurs carquois pour nous mettre en asseurance, ils y entrerent et nous firent approcher de
terre, où nous debarquâmes non pas sans crainte de
nostre part. il fallut au commencement parler par
gestes, parceque personne n'entendoit rien de six
langues que je scavois, il se trouva enfin un viellard
qui parloit un peu L'Ilinois.

Nous leurs fîmes paroistre par nos presens que
nous allions a la mer, ils entendirent bien ce que
nous Leur voulions dire, mais je ne scay s'ils con-
çeurent ceque je leurs dis de Dieu et des choses de
leur salut, c'est une semence jettée en terre qui fruc-
tifira en son temps. Nous n'eusmes point d'autre
reponse sinon que nous apprendrions tous ce que nous
desirions d'un aultre grand village nommé Akamsea
qui n'estoit qu'a 8 ou 10 lieuës plus bas, ils nous
presenterent de la sagamité et du poisson, et nous
passâmes La nuict chez eux avec assez d'inquietude.

SECTION 9ᵉᵐᵉ. RECEPTION QU'ON FAIT AUX FRANCOIS
DANS LA DERNIERE DES BOURGADES QU'ILS ONT
VEUËS. LES MŒURS & FAÇONS DE FAIRE DE CES
SAUVAGES. RAISONS POUR NE PAS PASSER OUTRE.

Nous embarquames le lendemain de grand matins
avec nostre interprette; un canot ou estoient
dix sauvages alloit un peu devant nous; estant arrivés a une demie lieuë des Akamsea, nous vismes

speak by signs, because none of them understood the
six languages which I spoke.   At last, we found an
old man who could speak a little Ilinois.

We informed them, by our presents, that we were
going to the sea.   They understood very well what
we wished to say to Them, but I know not whether
they apprehended what I told them about God, and
about matters pertaining to their salvation.   This is
a seed cast into the ground, which will bear fruit in
its time.   We obtained no other answer than that we
would learn all that we desired at another large village, called Akamsea, which was only 8 or 10 leagues
lower down.   They offered us sagamité and fish,
and we passed The night among them, with some
anxiety.

SECTION 9TH.   RECEPTION GIVEN TO THE FRENCH
    IN THE LAST VILLAGE WHICH THEY SAW.   THE
       MANNERS AND CUSTOMS OF THOSE SAVAGES.
          REASONS FOR NOT GOING FARTHER.

W E embarked early on the following day, with
our interpreter; a canoe containing ten savages went a short distance ahead of us.   When we
arrived within half a league of the Akamsea,[39] we
saw two canoes coming to meet us.   He who com-
manded stood upright, holding in his hand The calumet, with Which he made various signs, according
to the custom of the country.   He joined us, singing
very agreeably, and gave us tobacco to smoke; after
that, he offered us sagamité, and bread made of
indian corn, of which we ate a little.   He then
preceded us, after making us a sign to follow Him
slowly.   A place had been prepared for us under
The scaffolding of the chief of the warriors; it was

paroistre deux cânotz qui venoient au devant de nous :
Celuy qui y commandoit estoit debout tenant en
main Le calumet, avec Lequel il faisoit plusieurs
gestes selon la coustume du paÿs, il vint nous joindre
en chantant assez agreablement, et nous donna a
fumer, apres quoy il nous presenta de la sagamité et
du pain fait de bled d'inde, dont nous mangeammes
un peu ; Ensuitte il prit le devant nous ayant fait
signe de venir doucement apres Luy : on nous avoit
preparé un place sous L'eschaffault du chef des guerriers, elle estoit propre et tapissée de belles nattes
de jonc, sur Lesquelles on nous fit asseoir, ayant
autour de nous les anciens, qui estoient plus proches ;
apres Les guerriers et enfin tout Le peuple en foule.
Nous trouvâmes là par bonheur un Jeune homme
qui entendoit L'Ilinois beaucoup mieux que L'Interprette que nous avions amené de Mitchigamea, ce fut
par son moyen que je parlay d'abord a toute cette
assemblée par Les presens ordinaires : ils admiroient
ce que je Leurs disois de Dieu et des mysteres de
nostre s^{te} foy ; ils faisoient paroistre un grand desir
de me retenir avec eux pour Les pouvoir instruire

Nous leurs demandâmes ensuitte ce qu'ils scavoient
de la mer ; ils nous repondirent que nous n'en estions
qu'a dix journées ; nous aurions pû faire ce chemin
en 5 jours ; qu'ils ne connoissoient pas Les Nations
qui L'habitoient a cause que Leurs ennemys Les
empechoient d'avoir Commerce avec ces Europeans,
que les haches, Cousteaux, et rassade que nous voions
Leur estoient vendues en partie par des Nations de
L'est, et en partie par une bourgade D'Ilinois placée
a L'ouest a quatre journées de la ; que ces sauvages
que nous avons rencontrés qui avoient des fusils

clean, and carpeted with fine rush mats. Upon
These we were made to sit, having around us the
elders, who were nearest to us; after them, The warriors; and, finally, all The common people in a crowd.
We fortunately found there a Young man who understood Ilinois much better than did The Interpreter
whom we had brought from Mitchigamea. Through
him, I spoke at first to the whole assembly by The
usual presents. They admired what I said to Them
about God and the mysteries of our holy faith.
They manifested a great desire to retain me among
them, that I might instruct Them.

We afterward asked them what they knew about
the sea. They replied that we were only ten days'
journey from it — we could have covered the distance
in 5 days; that they were not acquainted with The
Nations who dwelt There, because Their enemies
prevented Them from Trading with those Europeans;
that the hatchets, Knives, and beads that we saw
were sold to Them partly by Nations from The east,
and partly by an Ilinois village situated at four days'
journey from their village westward. They also
told us that the savages with guns whom we had
met were Their Enemies, who barred Their way to
the sea, and prevented Them from becoming acquainted with the Europeans, and from carrying on
any trade with them; that, moreover, we exposed
ourselves to great dangers by going farther, on
account of the continual forays of their enemies along
the river, — because, as they had guns and were very
warlike, we could not without manifest danger
proceed down the river, which they constantly
occupy.

During this conversation, food was continually

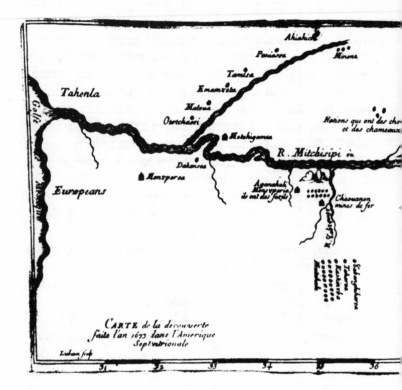

Carte de la decouverte faite l'an 1673 dans l'Amerique Septvntrionale

THEVEN

| Published by him

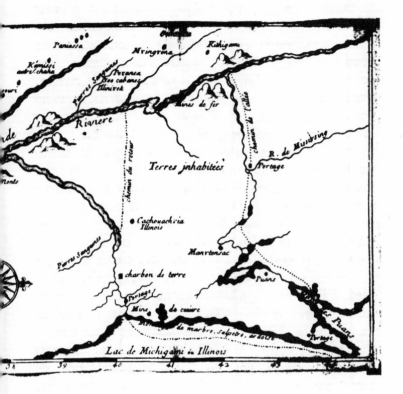

P, 1681

hat of Marquette.]

estoient Leurs Ennemys, lesquels Leurs fermoient
le passage de la mer, et Les empechoient d'avoir
connoissance des Europeans, et d'avoir avec eux
aucun commerce; qu'au reste nous nous exposions
beau coup de passer plus oultre a cause des courses
continuelles que leurs ennemys font sur la riviere,
qui ayant des fusils et estant fort agguerris, nous ne
pouvions pas sans un danger evident avancer sur
cette riviere qu'ils occupent continuellement.

Pendant cet entretien, on nous apportoit continuellement a manger dans de grands platz de bois,
tantost de la sagamité, tantost du bled entier, tantost
d'un morceaux de chien, toute La journée se passa
en festins.   Ces peuples sont assez officieux et liberaux de ce qu'ils ont, mais ils sont miserable pour
Le vivre, nosant aller a la chasse des bœufs sauvages
a cause de Leurs Ennemys, il est vray qu'ils ont le
bled d'inde en abondance, qu'ils sement en toutes
saisons, nous en vismes en mesme temps qui estoient
en maturité. D'autre qui ne faisoit que pousser, et
l'autre qui estoit en Laict, de sorte qu'ils sement trois
fois l'an.   Ils le font cuire dans de grands potz de
terre qui sont fort bien faits. ils ont aussi des
assiétes de terres cuitte dontz ils se servent a divers
usages.   les hommes vont nuds, portant Les cheveux
courtz; ont le néz percé d'ou pend de la rassade
aussi bien que de Leurs oreilles: les femmes sont
vestues de meschantes peaux, noüent Leurs cheveux
en deux tresses qu'elles jettent derriere les oreilles,
et n'ont aucune rareté pour se parer.   Leurs festins
se font sans aucune ceremonie, ils presentent aux In-
vitez de grand platz dontz chascun mange a discretion, et se donnent les restes, Les uns aux autres.

brought to us in large wooden platters, consisting
sometimes of sagamité, sometimes of whole corn,
sometimes of a piece of dog's flesh. The entire day
was spent in feasting. These people are very
obliging and liberal with what they have; but
they are wretchedly provided with food, for they
dare not go and hunt wild cattle, on account of
Their Enemies. It is true that they have an
abundance of indian corn, which they sow at all
seasons. We saw at the same time some that
was ripe, some other that had only sprouted, and
some again in the Milk, so that they sow it three
times a year. They cook it in great earthern jars,
which are very well made.⁴⁰ They have also plates
of baked earth which they use in various ways.
The men go naked, and wear Their hair short; they
pierce their noses, from which, as well as from Their
ears, hang beads. The women are clad in wretched
skins; they knot Their hair in two tresses which
they throw behind their ears, and have no ornaments
with which to adorn themselves. Their feasts are
given without any ceremony. They offer the
Guests large dishes, from which all eat at discretion
and offer what is left to one another. Their language
is exceedingly difficult, and I could succeed in pronouncing only a few words notwithstanding all my
efforts. Their Cabins, which are made of bark, are
Long and Wide; they sleep at the two ends, which
are raised two feet above the ground. They keep
Their corn in large baskets made of Canes, or in
gourds as large as half-barrels. They know nothing
of the Beaver. Their wealth consists in the skins
of wild cattle. They never see snow in their country, and recognize The winter only through The

Leur langue est extremement difficile, et je ne pouvois venir about d'en prononcer quelques motz, quelque effort que je pusse faire. Leurs Cabannes qui sont faites d'escorce sont Longues et Larges, ils couchent au deux boutz, elevez de deux pieds de terre; Ils y gardent Leurs bled dans de grands pannier faits de Cannes ou dans des gourdes grosses comme des demy bariques. Ils ne scavent ce que c'est que le Castor. Leurs richesses consistent en peaux de bœufs sauvages; ils ne voient jamais de neige chez eux, et ne connoissent L'hyver que par Les pluyës qui y tombent plus souvent qu'en esté; nous n'y avons pas mangé de fruictz que des melons d'eau. S'ils scavoient cultiver leur terre, ils en auroient de toutes les sortes.

Le soir les anciens firent un conseil secret dans le dessein que quelqu'uns avoient de nous casser la teste pour nous piller, mais le Chef rompit toutes ces menées — nous ayant envoyé querir pour marque de parfaitte asseurance il dansa le calumet devant nous, de la façons que j'ay descript cy dessus, et pour nous oster toute crainte, il m'en fit present.

Nous fismes Mr Jolliet et Moy un aultre Conseil, pour deliberer sur ce que nous avions a faire si nous pousserions oultre ou si nous nous contenterions de la decouverte que nous avions faite. Apres avoir attentivement consideré que nous n'estions pas loing du golphe Mexique dont le bassin estant a la haulteur de 31 degrez 60 minutes, et nous nous trouvant a 33, 40 minutes, nous ne pouvions pas en estre eloignez plus de 2 ou 3 journées qu'indubitablement la riviere Missisipi avoit sa decharge dans la floride ou golphe Mexique, n'on pas du costé de L'est dans la Vir-

rains, which there fall more frequently than in summer. We ate no other fruit there than watermelons. If they knew how to till their soil, they would have fruits of all kinds.

In the evening, the elders held a secret council, in regard to the design entertained by some to break our heads and rob us; but the Chief put a stop to all these plots. After sending for us, he danced the calumet before us, in the manner I have already described, as a token of our entire safety; and, to relieve us of all fear, he made me a present of it.

Monsieur Jolliet and I held another Council, to deliberate upon what we should do—whether we should push on, or remain content with the discovery which we had made. After attentively considering that we were not far from the gulf of Mexico, the basin of which is at the latitude of 31 degrees 60 minutes, while we were at 33 degrees 40 minutes, we judged that we could not be more than 2 or 3 days' journey from it; and that, beyond a doubt, the Missisipi river discharges into the florida or Mexican gulf, and not to The east in Virginia, whose sea-coast is at 34 degrees latitude,—which we had passed, without, however, having as yet reached the sea,—or to the west in California, because in that case our route would have been to The west, or the west-southwest, whereas we had always continued It toward the south. We further considered that we exposed ourselves to the risk of losing the results of this voyage, of which we could give no information if we proceeded to fling ourselves into the hands of the Spaniards who, without doubt, would at least have detained us as captives. Moreover, we saw very plainly that we were not in a condition to resist Savages allied to

ginie, dont le bord de la mer est a 34 degréz que
nous avons passéz sans neanmoins estre encor arrivés
a la mer, non pas aussi du costé de l'oüest a la Californie, parceque nous devions pour cela avoir nostre
route a L'ouest, oú a l'oüest soroüest et nous L'avons
tousjour en au sud. Nous considerâmes de plus que
nous nous exposions a perdre la fruict de ce voyage
duquel nous ne pourrions pas donner aucune connoissance, si nous allions nous jetter entre les mains des
Espagnols qui sans doubte nous auroient du moins
retenus captifs. En oultre, nous voyons bien que
nous n'estions pas en estat de resister a des Sauvages
allies Les Europeans, nombreux, et experts a tirer
du fusil qui infestoient continuellement le bas de
cette riviere. Enfin, nous avions pris toutes les connoissances qu'on peut souhaiter dans cette decouverte
toutes ces raisons firent conclure pour Le Retour,
que vous declarames aux sauvages et pour lequel
nous nous preparâmes apres un jour de repos.

SECTION DIXIÉME. RETOUR DU PERE ET DES FRAN-
    COIS. BAPTEME D'UN ENFANT MORIBOND.

APRES un mois du Navigation en descendant sur
    Missisipi depuis le 42ᵈ degré jusqu'au 34ᵉ et
plus, et apres avoir publié l'Evangile, autant que j'ay
pû, aux Nations que j'ay rencontrées, nous partons
le 17ᵉ Juillet du village des akensea pour retourner
sur nos pas. Nous remontons donc a Missisipi qui
nous donne bien de la peine a refouler ses Courans,
il est vray que nous le quittons vers les 38ᵉ degrés
pour entrer dans une aultre riviere qui nous abbrege
de beaucoup Le chemin et nous conduit avec peu de
peine dans le lac des Ilinois

The Europeans, who were numerous, and expert in firing guns, and who continually infested the lower part of the river. Finally, we had obtained all the information that could be desired in regard to this discovery. All these reasons induced us to decide upon Returning; this we announced to the savages, and, after a day's rest, made our preparations for it.

SECTION TENTH. RETURN OF THE FATHER AND OF THE FRENCH. BAPTISM OF A DYING CHILD.

AFTER a month's Navigation, while descending Missisipi from the 42nd to the 34th degree, and beyond, and after preaching the Gospel as well as I could to the Nations that I met, we start on the 17th of July from the village of the akensea, to retrace our steps. We therefore reascend the Missisipi which gives us much trouble in breasting its Currents. It is true that we leave it, at about the 38th degree, to enter another river, which greatly shortens our road, and takes us with but little effort to the lake of the Ilinois.

We have seen nothing like this river that we enter, as regards its fertility of soil, its prairies and woods; its cattle, elk, deer, wildcats, bustards, swans, ducks, parroquets, and even beaver. There are many small lakes and rivers. That on which we sailed is wide, deep, and still, for 65 leagues. In the spring and during part of The summer there is only one portage of half a league.[41] We found on it a village of Ilinois called Kaskasia, consisting of 74 Cabins. They received us very well, and obliged me to promise that I would return to instruct them. One of the chiefs of this nation, with his young men, escorted us to the Lake of the Ilinois, whence, at last, at The

Nous n'avons rien vue de semblable a cette riviere où nous entrons pour la bonté de terres, des prairies, des bois, des bœufs, des cerfs, des chevreux, des chatz sauvages, des outardes, des cygnes, des canards, des perroquetz, et mesmes des castors, il y a quantité de petitz lacs, et de petites rivieres. Celle sur laquelle nous navigeons est large, profonde, paisible, pendant 65 lieues, le printemps et une partie de L'este on ne fait de transport que pendant une demi lieuë. Nous y trouvâmes une bourgade d'Ilinois nommé Kaskasia composée de 74 Cabanes, ils nous y ont tres bien receus, et ils m'ont obligé de leur promettre que je retournerois pour les instruire. Un des chefs de cette nation, avec sa jeunesse, nous est venu conduire jusqu'au Lac des Ilinois d'ou enfin nous nous sommes rendus dans la baye des puantz sur La fin de Septembre, d'ou nous estions partis vers le commencement de Juin.

Quand tout ce voyage n'auroit causé que le salut d'une ame, j'estimerois toutes mes peines bien recompensées, et c'est ce que jay sujet de presumer, car lorsque ie retournois nous passames par les Ilinois de Peȣarea je fus trois jours a leur publier la foÿ dans toutes leurs cabanes, apres quoy comme nous nous embarquions, on m'apporta au bord de L'eau un enfant moribond que je baptisay un peu avant qu'il mourut par une providence admirable pour le salut de cette ame Innocente.

end of September, we reached the bay des puantz, from which we had started at the beginning of June.

Had this voyage resulted in the salvation of even one soul, I would consider all my troubles well rewarded, and I have reason to presume that such is the case. For, when I was returning, we passed through the Ilinois of Peouarea,[42] and during three days I preached the faith in all their Cabins; after which, while we were embarking, a dying child was brought to me at The water's edge, and I baptized it shortly before it died, through an admirable act of providence for the salvation of that Innocent soul.

Journal incomplet du P. Jacques Marquette,
adressé au R. P. Claude Dablon,
supérieur des Missions.

+

Mon Reuerend Pere.
Pax X¹.

Ayant este contraint de demeurer a f̔. François tout l'este, acaufe de quelque incommodite, en
ayant este guery dez le mois de feptembre, I'y attendois l'arriuee de nos gens au retour de la bas pour
fçauoir ceque ie ferois pour mon hyuernement; lefquels m'en apporterent les ordres pour mon uoyage a
la miffion de la Conception des Ilinois, ayant fatiffait
aux fentiments de V R pour les coppies de mon iournal touchant la Riuiere de miffifipi, Ie partis auec
Pierre Porteret et Iacque [*blank space in MS.*] le 25
oct 1674 fur les midy le uent nous contraignit de
coucher a la fortie de la Riuiere ou les Pȣteȣatamis
f'affembloient, les anciens n'ayant pas uoulu qu'on
allaft du coftez des Ilinois, de peur que la ieuneffe
amaffant des robbes auec les marchandifes qu'ils ont
apportez de la bas, et chaffant au Caftor ne uoulut
defcendre le printemps qu'ils croient auoir fuiet de
craindre les nadȣeffi

paffant au uillage nous ny trouuafmes plus que
deux cabannes qui partoient pour aller hyuerner a
la gafparde, nous apprifmes que 5 canots de Pȣteȣatamis et 4 d Ilinois estoient partis pour aller aux
Kafkafkia.

Unfinished Journal of Father Jacques Marquette,
addressed to the Reverend Father Claude
Dablon, superior of the Missions.

+

M Y REVEREND FATHER,
        Pax Christi.
        Having been compelled to remain at st.
Francois throughout the summer on account of an
ailment, of which I was cured in the month of september, I awaited there the return of our people from
down below, in order to learn what I was to do with
regard to my wintering. They brought me orders
to proceed to the mission of la Conception among the
Ilinois. After complying with Your Reverence's
request for copies of my journal concerning the
missisipi River, I departed with Pierre Porteret and
Jacque [*blank space in MS.*], on the 25th of october,
1674, about noon. The wind compelled us to pass
the night at the outlet of the River, where the Poutewatamis were assembling; for the elders would not
allow them to go in the direction of the Ilinois, lest
the young men, after collecting robes with the goods
that they brought from below, and after hunting
Beaver, might seek to go down in the spring; because
they have reason to fear the nadouessi.

On passing the village, we found only two cabins *26th of* *october.*
of savages, who were going to spend the winter at la
gasparde. We learned that 5 canoes of Poutewatamis, and 4 of Ilinois, had started to go to the
Kaskaskia.

nous fufmes arreftez le matin par la pluye, nous eufmes beau temps et calme l'aprefdifnée que nous rencontrafmes dans l'ance a l'efturgeon les fauuages qui marchoient deuant nous

on arriue au portage, un canot qui auoit pris le deuant eft caufe que qu'on ne tue point de gibier; nous commençons notre portage et allons coucher de l'autre bord, ou le mauuais temps nous fift bien de la peine   Pierre n'arriue qu'a une heure de nuit f'efgarant par d'un fentier ou il n'auoit iamais efte, apres la pluye et le tonnerre, il tombe de la neige.

ayant efte contraint de changer de cabannage, on continue de porter les paquets, le portage a pres d'une lieuë, et affez incommode en plufieurs endroits, les Ilinois f'eftant affemblez le foir dans notre cabanne demandent, qu'on ne les quitte pas, comme nous pouuions auoir befoin d'eux et qu'ils connoiffent mieux le lac que nous, on leur promet

les femmes Ilinoifes acheuent le matin notre portage, on est arreste par le uent   il n'y a point de beftes

on parte par un affez beau temps, et l'on uient coucher a une petite riuiere.   le chemin de l'ance a l'efturgeon par terre est tres difficile, nous n'en marchions pas loing l'automne paffe, lorfque nous entrafmes dans le bois

Ayant dit la fte. meffe on uient coucher dans une riuiere, d'ou l'on ua aux Pꝰteꝰatamis par un beau chemin; chachagꝰeffiꝰ Ilinois fort confidere parmy fa nation, a raifon en partie qu il fe mefle des affaires de la traitte arriue la nuit auec un cheureux fur fon dos, dont il nous fait part.

We were delayed in the morning by rain; in the *27.*
afternoon, we had fine, calm weather, so that at sturgeon bay we joined the savages, who traveled ahead
of us.

We reached the portage.[48]   A canoe that had gone *28.*
ahead prevented us from killing any game.   We
began our portage and slept on the other shore,
where the stormy weather gave us much trouble.
Pierre did not arrive until an hour after dark, having lost his way on a path where he had never been.
After the rain and thunder, snow fell.

Being compelled to change our camping-ground, *29.*
we continue to carry our packs.   The portage covers
nearly a league, and is very difficult in many places.
The Ilinois assemble in the evening in our cabin,
and ask us not to leave them, as we may need them,
and they know the lake better than we do.   We
promise them this.

The Ilinois women complete our portage in the *30.*
morning.   We are delayed by the wind.   There are
no animals.

We start, with tolerably fair weather, and sleep at *31.*
a small river.   The road by land from sturgeon bay
is very difficult.   Last autumn, we were traveling
not far from it when we entered the forest.

After I said holy mass, we came for the night to *November*
a river, whence one goes to the Poutewatamis by a *1.*
good road.   Chachagwessiou, an Ilinois greatly
esteemed among his nation, partly because he en-
gages in the fur trade, arrived at night with a deer
on his back, of which he gave us a share.

After holy mass, we travel all day in very fine *2.*
weather.   We kill two cats, which are almost nothing but fat.

La fᵗᵉ. meſſe dit, nous marchons toute la iournee par un fort beau temps, on tuë deux chats qui n'ont quaſi que de la graiſſe

comme i'estois par terre marchant ſur le beau ſable tout le bord de l'eau eſtoit d'herbes ſemblables a celles qu'on peſche aux retz a fᵗ. Ignace, mais ne pouuant paſſer une riuiere, nos gens y entrent pour m'embarquer mais on n'en put ſortir acauſe de la lame, tous les autres canots paſſent a la reſerue d'un ſeul qui uient auec nous

on est arreste   Il y a apparence qu'il y a quelque Iſle au large le gibier y paſſant le ſoir

nous euſmes aſſez de peine de ſortir de la Riuiere ſur le midy, on trouua les ſauuages dans une riuiere, ou ie pris occaſion d'inſtruire les Ilinois, a raiſon d'un feſtin que naʊaſkingʊe uenoit de faire a une peau de loup.

on fiſt une belle iournée, les ſauuages eſtant a la chaſſe deſcouurirent quelques piſtes dhommes cequi oblige d'arreſter le lendemain

on mit a terre ſur les 2 heures acauſe d'un beau cabannage, ou l'on fuſt arreſte 5 iours, acauſe de la grande agitation du lac ſans aucun uent enſuitte par la neige, qui fuſt le lendemain fonduë par le ſoleil et un uent du large.

apres auoir fait aſſez de chemin on cabanne dans un bel endroit ou l'on eſt arreſte 3 iours Pierre raccommode le fuzil d'un ſauuage, neige tombe, la nuit et fond le iour

on couche aux equors aſſez mal cabannez   les ſauuages demeurent derriere durant qu'on eſt arreſte du uent 2 iours et demy Pierre allant dans le bois trouue la prairie a 20 lieues du portage, il paſſe auſſi

While I am ashore, walking on fine sand,—the   *3.*
whole water's edge being covered with grass similar
to that which is hauled up by the nets at st. Ignace,—
I come to a river which I am unable to cross. Our
people enter it, in order to take me on board; but
we are unable to go out, on account of the waves.
All the other canoes go on, excepting one, which
came with us.

We are delayed. There seems to be an Island out   *4.*
in the lake, for the game go there at night.

We had considerable difficulty in getting out of the   *5.*
River at noon. We found the savages in a river, where   *↳*
I seized the opportunity of instructing the Ilinois,
on account of a feast that nawaskingwe had just
given to a wolfskin.

We performed a good day's journey. While the   *6.*
savages were hunting, they discovered some tracks
of men, and this compelled us to stay over on the
following day.

We landed about 2 o'clock, because there was a   *9.*
good camping-ground. We were detained there for
5 days, on account of the great agitation of the lake,
although without any wind; and afterward of the
snow, which was melted on the following day by the
sun, and a breeze from the lake.

After proceeding a sufficient distance, we camp at   *15.*
a favorable place, where we are detained 3 days.
Pierre mends a savage's gun. Snow falls at night,
and thaws during the day.

We sleep near the bluffs, and are very poorly   *20.*
sheltered. The savages remain behind while we
are delayed 2 days and a half by the wind. Pierre
goes into the woods, and finds the prairie 20 leagues
from the portage. He also goes through a fine canal

fur un beau canal comme en voute haut de la hauteur d'un homme, ou il y auoit un pied d'eau

23 eftant embarque fur le midy nous eufmes affez de
peine de gagner une riuiere, le froid commença pour
lors, et plus d'un pied de neige couurit la terre qui eft
toufiours depuis demeure, on fuft arreste la 3 iours
durant lefquels Pierre tua un cheureux 3 outardes
et 3 cocqs d'Inde qui estoient fort bons, les autres
pafferent iufques aux prairies, un fauuage ayant
defcouuert quelques cabannes nous uint trouuer,
Iacques y alla le lendemain auec luy 2 chaffeurs me
uinrent auffi uoir, c'eftoient des mafkꙋtens au nombre de 8 ou 9 cabannes, lefquelles f'eftoient feparez
les uns des autres pour pouuoir uiure, auec des
fatigues prefque impoffibles a des françois ils
marchent tout lhyuer, dans des chemins tres difficiles, les terres eftant plaines de ruiffeaux de petits
lacs et de marefts, ils font tres mal cabannez, et
mangent ou ieufnent felon les lieux ou ils se rencon-
trent; eftant arrefte par le uent nous remarquafmes
qu'il y auoit de grandes battures au large ou la lame
brifoient continuellement: ce fuft la que ie fentis
quelque atteinte d'un flux de uentre.

27 nous eusmes affez de peine de fortir de la riuiere,
et ayant fait enuiron 3 lieues nous trouuafmes les
fauuages qui auoient tuez des bœufs, et 3 ilinois qui
eftoient uenu du uillage, nous fufmes arreftez la
d'un uent de terre des lames prodigieufes qui uenoient
du large, et du froid,

Decembre
1 on deuance les fauuages pour pouuoir dire la
f^te. meffe,

3 ayant dit la f^te. meffe eftant embarque nous
fufmes contrains de gagner une pointe pour pouuoir
mettre a terre acaufe des bourguignons

which is vaulted, as it were, to the height of a man, in which there is water a foot deep.

After embarking at noon, we experienced some difficulty in reaching a river. Then the cold began, and more than a foot of snow covered the ground; it has remajned ever since. We were delayed for 3 days, during which Pierre killed a deer, 3 bustards, and 3 Turkeys, which were very good. The others proceeded to the prairies. A savage discovered some cabins, and came to get us. Jacques went there on the following day, with him; 2 hunters also came to see me. They were maskoutens, to the number of 8 or 9 cabins, who had separated from the others in order to obtain subsistence. With fatigues almost impossible to frenchmen, they travel throughout the winter over very bad roads, the land abounding in streams, small lakes, and swamps. Their cabins are wretched; and they eat or starve, according to the places where they happen to be. Being detained by the wind, we noticed that there were great shoals out in the lake, over which the waves broke continually. Here I had an attack of diarrhœa.

23.

We had some trouble in getting out of the river; then, after proceeding about 3 leagues, we found the savages, who had killed some cattle, and 3 ilinois who had come from the village. We were delayed there by a wind from the land, by heavy waves from the lake, and by cold.

27.

We went ahead of the savages, so that I might celebrate holy mass.

December 1.

After saying holy mass, we embarked, and were compelled to make for a point, so that we could land, on account of floating masses of ice.

3.

4   nous partifmes heureufement pour uenir a la
riuiere du portage qui eftoit gelee d'un demy pied,
ou il y auoit plus de neige que par tout ailleurs,
comme auffi plus de pifte de beftes et de cocqs
dInde.

La nauigation du lac eft affez belle d'un portage a
l'autre, n y ayant aucune trauerfe a faire, et pouuant
mettre a terre par tout, moyennant qu'on ne foit point
opiniaftre a uouloir marcher dans les lames et de
grand uent, les terres qui le bordent ne ualent
rien, excepte quand on eft aux prairies, on trouue 8
ou 10 riuieres affez belles, la chaffe du cheureux eft
tres belle a mefure qu'on f'efloigne des Pꙋteꙋatamis,

12.   comme on commençoit hier a traifner pour approcher du portage les Ilinois ayant quittez les Pꙋteꙋatamis arriuerent auec bien de la peine nous ne
pufmes dire la fᵗᵉ. meffe le iour de la Conception
acaufe du mauuais temps et du froid, durant notre
feiour a l'entree de la riuiere Pierre et Iacques
tuerent 3 bœufs et 4 cheureux dont l'un courut affez
loing ayant le cœur couppe en 2. on fe contenta de
tuer 3 ou 4 cocqs d'inde de plufieurs qui uenoient
autour de notre cabanne, parcequ'ils mouroient quafi
perdrix.   de faim; Iacques apporta une perdrix qu'il auoit
tuez, femblable en tout a celles de France, excepte
qu'elle auoit comme deux aiflerons de 3 ou 4 aifles
longues d'un doigt proche la tefte, dont elles cou-
urent les 2 coftez du col ou il n'y a point de plume

14.   estant cabannez proche le portage a 2 lieues dans
la riuiere nous refolufmes d'hyuerner la estant dans
l'impoffibilite de paffer outre estant trop embar-
raffe, et mon incommodite ne me permettant pas de
beaucoup fatiguer. plufieurs Ilinois pafferent hier

We started with a favoring wind, and reached the   *4.*
river of the portage, which was frozen to the depth
of half a foot; there was more snow there than else-
where, as well as more tracks of animals and Turkeys.

Navigation on the lake is fairly good from one
portage to the other, for there is no crossing to be
made, and one can land anywhere, unless one persist
in going on when the waves are high and the wind is
strong. The land bordering it is of no value, except
on the prairies. There are 8 or 10 quite fine rivers.
Deer-hunting is very good, as one goes away from
the Poutewatamis.

As we began yesterday to haul our baggage in   *12.*
order to approach the portage, the Ilinois who had
left the Poutewatamis arrived, with great difficulty.
We were unable to celebrate holy mass on the day
of the Conception, owing to the bad weather and
cold. During our stay at the entrance of the river,
Pierre and Jacques killed 3 cattle and 4 deer, one of
which ran some distance with its heart split in 2.
We contented ourselves with killing 3 or 4 turkeys,
out of many that came around our cabin because they
were almost dying of hunger. Jacques brought in
a partridge that he had killed, exactly like those of   *Partridge.*
France except that it had two ruffs, as it were, of
3 or 4 feathers as long as a finger, near the head,
covering the 2 sides of the neck where there are
no feathers.

Having encamped near the portage, 2 leagues up   *14.*
the river, we resolved to winter there, as it was impossible to go farther, since we were too much hin-
dered and my ailment did not permit me to give myself much fatigue. Several Ilinois passed yesterday,
on their way to carry their furs to nawaskingwe;

pour aller porter leur pelleterie a naϫafᴋingϫe, auf-
quels on donne un bœufs et un cheureux que Iacque
auoit tué le iour d'auparauant, ie ne penſe pas auoir
ueu de ſauuage plus affamé de petun François qu'eux,
ils uinrent ietter a nos pieds des caſtors pour en
auoir quelque bout, mais nous leur rendiſmes en leur
en donnant quelque pipe parceque nous n'auions pas
encore conclu ſi nous paſſerions outre,

15   Chachagϫeſſiϫ et les autres Ilinois nous quitterent
pour aller trouuer leur gens, et leur donner les
marchandiſes qu'ils auoient apportez pour auoir leur
robbes en quoy ils ſe gouuernent comme les trait-
teurs, et ne donnent guere plus que les François; ie
les inſtruiſis auant leur depart, remettant au printemps de tenir conſeil quand ie ferois au uillage; ils
nous traitterent 3 belles robbes de bœuf pour une
coudee de petun, leſquelles nous ont beaucoup ferui
cet hyuer, eſtant ainſi deſbaraſſez, nous difmes La
meſſe de la Conception: depuis le 14 mon incommodite ſe tourna en flux de ſang.

30   Iacque arriua du uillage des Ilinois qui n'eſtoit
qu'a ſix lieues d'icy ou ils auoient faim le froid et la
neige les empeſchant de chaſſer, quelques uns ayant
aduerti la Toupine et le chirurgien que nous eſtions
icy, et ne pouuant quitter leur cabanne auoient tellement donnez la peur aux ſauuages croyant que nous
aurions faim demeurant icy que Iacque euſt bien de
la peine d'empeſcher 15 ieunes gens de uenir pour
emporter toute notre affaire.

*Januier
1675
16.*   Auſſitoſt que les 2 françois ſceurent que mon mal
m'empeſchoit d'aller chez eux le chirurgien uint icy
auec un ſauuage pour nous apporter des bluets et du
bled; ils ne font qu'a 18 lieues d'icy dans un beau

we gave them one of the cattle and one of the deer that Jacque had killed on the previous day. I do not think that I have ever seen any savages more eager for French tobacco than they. They came and threw beaver-skins at our feet, to get some pieces of it; but we returned these, giving them some pipefuls of the tobacco because we had not yet decided whether we would go farther.

Chachagwessiou and the other Ilinois left us, to *15.* go and join their people and give them the goods that they had brought, in order to obtain their robes. In this they act like the traders, and give hardly any more than do the French. I instructed them before their departure, deferring the holding of a council until the spring, when I should be in their village. They traded us 3 fine robes of ox-skins for a cubit of tobacco; these were very useful to us during the winter. Being thus rid of them, we said The mass of the Conception. After the 14th, my disease turned into a bloody flux.

Jacque arrived from the Ilinois village, which is *30.* only six leagues from here; there they were suffering from hunger, because the cold and snow prevented them from hunting. Some of them notified la Tou- pine [44] and the surgeon that we were here; and, as they could not leave their cabin, they had so fright- ened the savages, believing that we would suffer from hunger if we remained here, that Jacque had much difficulty in preventing 15 young men from coming to carry away all our belongings.

As soon as the 2 frenchmen learned that my ill- *January,* ness prevented me from going to them, the surgeon *1675.* came here with a savage, to bring us some blueber- *16.* ries and corn. They are only 18 leagues from here,

lieu de chaſſe pour les bœufs et les cheureux et les
cocqs d'inde qui y ſont excellents, ils auoient auſſi
amaſſez des uiures en nous attendant; et auoient
fait entendre aux ſauuages que leur cabanne eſtoit a
la robbe noire, et on peut dire qu'ils ont fait et dit
tout ce qu'on pouuoit attendre d'eux; le chirurgien
ayant icy ſeiourne pour faire ſes deuotions; l'en-
uoyay Iacque auec luy pour dire aux Ilinois qui
eſtoient proche de la, que mon incommodite m'empeſchoit de les aller uoir, et que i'aurois meſme de la
peine d'y aller le printemps ſi elle continuoit

24   Iacque retourna, auec un ſac de bled et d'autres
rafraiſchiſſement que les François luy auoient donnez
pour moy: il apporta auſſi les langues et de la
uiande de deux bœufs qu'un ſauuage et luy auoient
tuez proches d'icy; mais toutes les beſtes ſe ſentent
du mauuais temps

26   3 Ilinois nous apporterent de la part des anciens 2
ſacs de bled de la uiande ſeche, des citrouïlles et 12
caſtors, 1°. pour me faire une natte, 2°. pour me
demander de la poudre, 3 pour que nous n'euſſions
pas faim, 4 pour auoir quelque peu de marchandiſes; ie leur reſpondis, 1nt. que i'eſtois uenu pour les
inſtruire, en leur parlant de la priere, &c. 2nt. que ie
ne leur donnerois point de poudre, puiſque nous taſ-
chions de mettre par tout la paix, et que ie ne uoulois
qu'ils commençaſſent la guerre avec les muiamis.
3nt. que nous n'apprehendions point la faim, 4nt.
que i'encouragerois les françois a leur apporter des
marchandiſes, et qu'il falloit qu'ils ſatiffiſſent ceux
qui eſtoient chez eux pour la raſſade qu'on leur auoit
pris, dez que le chirurgien fuſt party pour uenir icy.
comme ils eſtoient uenus de 20 lieuës, pour les payer

in a fine place for hunting cattle, deer, and turkeys, which are excellent there. They had also collected provisions while waiting for us; and had given the savages to understand that their cabin belonged to the black gown; and it may be said that they have done and said all that could be expected from them. After the surgeon had spent some time here, in order to perform his devotions, I sent Jacque with him to tell the Ilinois near that place that my illness prevented me from going to see them; and that I would even have some difficulty in going there in the spring, if it continued.

Jacque returned with a sack of corn and other deli- *24.* cacies, which the French had given him for me.   He also brought the tongues and flesh of two cattle, which a savage and he had killed near here.   But all the animals feel the bad weather.

3 Ilinois brought us, on behalf of the elders, 2 *26.* sacks of corn, some dried meat, pumpkins, and 12 beaver-skins: 1st, to make me a mat; 2nd, to ask me for powder; 3rd, that we might not be hungry; 4th, to obtain a few goods.   I replied: 1st, that I had come to instruct them, by speaking to them of prayer, etc.; 2nd, that I would give them no powder, because we sought to restore peace everywhere, and I did not wish them to begin war with the muiamis; 3rd, that we feared not hunger; 4th, that I would encourage the french to bring them goods, and that they must give satisfaction to those who were among them for the beads which they had taken as soon as the surgeon started to come here.   As they had come a distance of 20 leagues, I gave them, in order to reward them for their trouble and for what they had brought me, a hatchet, 2 knives, 3 clasp-knives,

de leur peine et de ce qu'ils m'auoient apportez ie
leur donnay une hache, 2 couteaux, 3 iambettes, 10
braffes de raffade, et 2 mirouirs doubles, et leur
difant que ie tafcherois d'aller au uillage feulement
pour quelques iours fi mon incommodite continuoit,
ils me dirent de prendre courage de demeurer et de
mourir dans leur pays et qu'on leur auoit dit que
i'y refterois pour longtemps

Feurier   Depuis que nous nous fommes addreffez a la f^te.
9.   Vierge Immaculée que nous auons commencez une
neufuaine par une meffe a laquelle Pierre et Iacque
qui font tout ce qu'ils peuuent pour me foulager
ont communiez pour demander a Dieu la fante, mon
flux de fang m'a quitte, il ne me refte qu'une foi-
bleffe d'eftomac, ie commence a me porter beaucoup
mieux et a reprendre mes forces; il ne cabanne d Ilinois qui f'eftoit rangee proche de nous depuis un
mois une partie ont repris le chemin des Pꝫt. et
quelques uns font encore au bord du lac ou ils
attendent que la nauigation foit libre ils emportent
des lettres pour nos P de f^t. François

20   nous auons eu le temps de remarquer les mareez
qui uiennent du lac lefquels hauffent et baiffent
Martes   plufieurs fois par iour et quoy qu'il n'y paroiffe
aucune abry dans le lac, on a ueu les glaces aller
contre le uent, ces mareez nous rendoient l'eau bonne
ou mauuaife parceque celle qui uient d'en hault coule
des prairies et de petits ruiffeaux, les cheureux qui
font en quantite uers le bord du lac font fi maigres
qu'on a este contraint d'en laiffer quelques uns de
ceux qu'on auoit tuez

Mars   on tue plufieurs perdrix dont il n'y a que les mals
23.
perdrix   qui ayent des aiflerons au col les femelles n'en

10 brasses of glass beads, and 2 double mirrors, telling them that I would endeavor to go to the village,—for a few days only, if my illness continued. They told me to take courage, and to remain and die in their country; and that they had been informed that I would remain there for a long time.

Since we addressed ourselves to the blessed Virgin Immaculate, and commenced a novena with a mass,— at which Pierre and Jacque, who do everything they can to relieve me, received communion,— to ask God to restore my health, my bloody flux has left me, and all that remains is a weakness of the stomach. I am beginning to feel much better, and to regain my strength. Out of a cabin of Ilinois, who encamped near us for a month, a portion have again taken the road to the Poutewatamis, and some are still on the lake-shore, where they wait until navigation is open. They bear letters for our Fathers of st. François.

February 9.

We have had opportunity to observe the tides coming in from the lake, which rise and fall several times a day; and, although there seems to be no shelter in the lake, we have seen the ice going against the wind. These tides made the water good or bad, because that which flows from above comes from prairies and small streams. The deer, which are plentiful near the lake-shore, are so lean that we had to abandon some of those which we had killed.

20.

Tides.

We killed several partridges, only the males of which had ruffs on the neck, the females not having any. These partridges are very good, but not like those of france.

March 23. Partridges.

ayant point ces perdrix font affez bonnes mais non
pas comme celles de france.

30.   le uent de nord ayant empefche le degel iufques
au 25 de Mars il commença par un uent de fud,   dez
le lendemain le gibier commença de paroiftre on
tua 30 tourtres que ie trouuay meilleures que celles
de la bas mais plus petites, tant les uieilles que les
ieunes; le 28 les glaces fe rompirent et f'arrefterent
au deffus de nous, le 29 les eaux courent si fort
que nous n'eufmes que le temps de defcabanner au
pluftot, mettre nos affaires fur des arbres, et tafcher
de chercher a coucher fur quelque but l'eau nous
gagnant prefque toute la nuit, mais ayant un peu gele,
et estant diminue comme nous estions aupres de nos
paquets, la digue uient de fe rompre, et les glaces a
f'efcouler et parceque les eaux remontent defia nous
allons nous embarquer pour continuer notre route

La f^te. Vierge Immaculee a pris un tel foin de nous
durant notre hyuernement que rien ne nous a manqué
pour les uiures, ayant encore un grand fac de bled de
refte de la uiande et de la graiffe; nous auons auffi
uefcu fort doucement, mon mal ne m'ayant point
empefche de dire la f^te. meffe tous les iours; nous
n'auons point pu garder du Carefme que les
Vendredys et famedys;

31   eftant hier party nous fifmes 3 lieues dans la
riuiere en remontant fans trouuer aucun portage, on
traifna peuteftre enuiron un demy arpant,   outre cette
defcharge la riuiere en a une autre par ou nous
debuons defcendre,   il n'y a que les terres bien hautes
qui ne foient point inondeez, celle ou nous fommes
a cru plus de 12 pieds   ce fut d'icy que nous com-
mençafmes notre portage Il y a 18 mois; les outardes

The north wind delayed the thaw until the   *30.*
25th of March, when it set in with a south wind.
On the very next day, game began to make its
appearance. We killed 30 pigeons, which I found
better than those down the great river; but they are
smaller, both old and young. On the 28th, the ice
broke up, and stopped above us. On the 29th, the
waters rose so high that we had barely time to
decamp as fast as possible, putting our goods in the
trees, and trying to sleep on a hillock. The water
gained on us nearly all night, but there was a slight
freeze, and the water fell a little, while we were near
our packages. The barrier has just broken, the ice
has drifted away; and, because the water is already
rising, we are about to embark to continue our
journey.

The blessed Virgin Immaculate has taken such
care of us during our wintering that we have not
lacked provisions, and have still remaining a large
sack of corn, with some meat and fat. We also
lived very pleasantly for my illness did not prevent
me from saying holy mass every day. We were
unable to keep Lent, except on Fridays and satur-
days.

We started yesterday and traveled 3 leagues up   *31.*
the river without finding any portage. We hauled
our goods probably about half an arpent. Besides
this discharge, the river has another one by which
we are to go down. The very high lands alone are
not flooded. At the place where we are, the water
has risen more than 12 feet. This is where we
began our portage 18 months Ago. Bustards and
ducks pass continually; we contented ourselves with
7. The ice, which is still drifting down, keeps us

et les canards paſſent continuellement on ſ'eſt
contente de 7, les glaces qui deriuent encore nous font
icy demeurer ne ſcachant pas en quel eſtat eſt le bas
de la riuiere

Auril

1

comme ie ne ſçay point encore ſi ie demeureray
cet eſte au uillage ou non acauſe de mon flux de
uentre, nous laiſſons icy une partie de ce dont nous
pouuons nous paſſer et ſur tout un ſac de bled   tandis
qu'un grand uent de ſud nous arreſte, nous eſperons
aller demain ou ſont les François, diſtant de 15
lieues d'icy

6.

les grands uents et le froid nous empeſchent de
marcher, les deux lacs par ou nous auons paſſez
ſont plains d'outardes d'oyes de canards de grues
et d'autres gibiers que nous ne connoiſſons point,
les rapides ſont aſſez dangereux en quelques
endroits, nous uenons de rencontrer le chirurgien
auec un ſauuage qui montoit auec une canottee de
pelleterie, mais le froid eſtant trop grand pour des
perſonnes qui ſont obligez de traiſner les canots dans
l'eau, il uient de faire cache de ſon caſtor et retourne
demain au uillage auec nous, ſi les François ont
des robbes de ce pays icy ils ne les defrobbent pas,
tant les fatigues ſont grandes pour les en tirer.

[Addressed: +

" A Mon Reuerend Pere Le P. Claude Dablon
Superieur des Miſſions dela Compagnie de Jesvs en
la nouuelle france   a quebec"]

[Endorsed: " Lettre et Iournal du feu P. Marquette."]

[Endorsed: " Tout ce qui regarde le voyage du
P Marquette "]

here, as we do not know in what condition the lower part of the river is.

As I do not yet know whether I shall remain next summer in the village, on account of my diarrhœa, we leave here part of our goods, those with which we can dispense, and especially a sack of corn. While a strong south wind delays us, we hope to go to-morrow to the place where the French are, at a distance of 15 leagues from here. *April 1.*

Strong winds and the cold prevent us from proceeding. The two lakes over which we passed are full of bustards, geese, ducks, cranes, and other game unknown to us. The rapids are quite dangerous in some places. We have just met the surgeon, with a savage who was going up with a canoe-load of furs; but, as the cold is too great for persons who are obliged to drag their canoes in the water, he has made a cache of his beaver-skins, and returns to the ᵛillage to-morrow with us. If the French procure robes in this country, they do not disrobe the savages, so great are the hardships that must be endured to obtain them. *6.*

[Addressed: +

" To My Reverend Father, Father Claude Dablon, Superior of the Missions of the Society of Jesus in new france. Quebec."]

[Endorsed: " Letter and Journal of the late Father Marquette."]

[Endorsed: " Everything concerning Father Marquette's voyage."]

Recit du second voyage et de la mort du P. Jacques Marquette.

L A mission des Ilinois fut establie en l'an 1674 apres le premier voyage que le pere jaques marquet fit pour descouurir de nouuelles terres et de nouueaux peuples qui sont sur la grande et fameuse riuiere apellèe missisipi

Il fit l'année d'apres vn second voyage pour y establir la mission, c'est ce qu'on va raconter.

SECTION 1ᴿᴱ. RECIT DU 2ᴰ VOYAGE QUE LE P MARQUET A FAICT AUX ILINOIS. IL Y ARRIUE NONOBSTANT SA MALADIE ET Y COMMENCE LA MISSION DE LA CONCEPTION.

L E P. Jaques marque*tte* ayant promis aux Ilinois au premier voyage qu'il fit ches eux en 1673 qu'il y retourneroit l'année suiuante poᵍ leur enseigner nos misteres, eut bien de la peine a tenir sa parolle. Les grandes fatigues de son premier voyage luy auoient Causé vn flux de sang, et l'auoient tellement abattu qu'il estoit hors d'esperance d'entreprendre vn second voyage. Cependant son mal ayant diminué et presque entierement Cessé sur la fin de l'esté de l'année suiuante, Il obtint permission de ses superieurs de retourner aux Ilinois poᵍ y donner commencement a cette belle mission.

Il partit pour cela dans le mois de nouembre de l'année 1674 de la baye des puants auec deux hoᵉˢ dont vn auoit desja faict le voyage auec luy; pendant vn

Account of the second voyage and the death of Father Jacques Marquette.

THE mission of the Ilinois was founded in the year 1674, after the first voyage which father jaques marquet made to discover new territories and new peoples who are on the great and famous river missisipi.

The year following, he made a second voyage in order to establish there the mission; it is that one which we are about to relate.

SECTION 1ST.   NARRATIVE OF THE 2ND VOYAGE THAT FATHER MARQUET MADE TO THE ILINOIS. HE REACHES THEM, NOTWITHSTANDING HIS ILLNESS, AND BEGINS THE MISSION OF LA CONCEPTION.

FATHER Jaques marquette, having promised the Ilinois on his first voyage to them, in 1673, that he would return to them the following year, to teach them the mysteries of our religion, had much difficulty in keeping his word.   The great hardships of his first voyage had Brought upon him a bloody flux, and had so weakened him that he was giving up the hope of undertaking a second.   However, his sickness decreased; and, as it had almost entirely Abated by the close of the summer in the following year, He obtained the permission of his superiors to return to the Ilinois and there begin that fair mission.

He set out for that purpose, in the month of november of the year 1674, from the bay des puanis,

mois de nauigation sur le lac des Ilinois il se porta
asses bien mais si tost que la neige Commenca a
tomber il fut repris de son flux de sang qui l'obligea
de s'arrester dans la riuiere qui Conduit aux Ilinois;
C'est la qu'ils firent vne Cabane po⁹ passer l'hyuer
auec de telles incomodités que son mal s'augmentant
de plus en plus, il vit bien que Dieu luy acordoit la
grace qu'il luy auoit tant de fois demandée, et mesme
il le dit tout simplement a ses deux Compagnons,
qu'asseurement il mourroit de cette maladie et dans
ce voyage.   Pour y bien disposer son ame malgré la
grande jndisposition de son Corps, il commenca vn
hyuernement si rude par les exercices de s^t. ignace
qu'il fit auec de grands sentiments de deuotion, et
beaucoup de Consolations Celestes, et puis il passa
tout le reste du temps a s'entretenir auec tout le
Ciel, n'ayant autre comerce auec la terre dans ces
deserts qu'auec ses deux Compagnons qu'il Confes-
soit et Communioit deux fois la sepmaine, et exhor-
toit autant que ses forces le pouuoient permettre
quelque temps apres noel po⁹ obtenir la grace de ne
pas mourir sans auoir pris possession de sa Chere
mission, il inuita ses Compagnons a faire vne neufuaine a l'honneur de l'imaculée conception de la s^{te}.
vierge; Il fut exaucé contre toutes les aparences
humaines, et se portant mieux il se mit en estat
d'aller au bourg des Ilinois si tost que la nauigation
seroit libre, ce qu'il fit auec bien de la Joye partant
po⁹ cela le 29 mars; il fut onze Jours en Chemin ou
il eut occasion de beaucoup souffrir, et pour sa propre
Indisposition n'estant pas entierement retabli, et par
vn temps tres rude et tres facheux.
    Estant enfin arriuée dans le bourg, il y fut receu

with two men, one of whom had made the former
voyage with him.   During a month of navigation on
the lake of the Ilinois, he was tolerably well; but,
as soon as the snow Began to fall, he was again
seized with his bloody flux, which compelled him to
halt in the river which Leads to the Ilinois.   It was
there that they constructed a Cabin in which to pass
the winter, amid such inconveniences that, his malady increasing more and more, he saw clearly that
God was granting to him the favor which he had
so many times besought from him; and he even told
his two Companions very plainly that he would
certainly die of that malady, and during that voyage.
Duly to prepare his soul, despite the severe indisposition of his Body, he began this so severe winter
sojourn by the retreat of st. ignatius, which he performed with every feeling of devotion, and many
Celestial Consolations; and then he passed the whole
of the remaining time in holding communion with
all Heaven,— having, in these deserts, no intercourse
with the earth except with his two Companions.   He
Confessed them and administered Communion to
them twice in the week, and exhorted them as much
as his strength permitted him.   A short time after
christmas, that he might obtain the favor of not
dying without having taken possession of his Dear
mission, he invited his Companions to make a novena
in honor of the immaculate conception of the blessed
virgin.   His prayer was answered, against all human
probability; and, his health improving, he prepared
himself to go to the village of the Ilinois as soon as
navigation should open,— which he did with much
Joy, setting out for that place on the 29th of march.
He spent eleven Days on the Way, during which time

comme vn ange du Ciel, et apres auoir assemblé par
diuerses fois les Chef de la nation auec tous les
anciens po⁹ ietter dans leurs esprits les premieres
semences de l'euangile; apres auoir porté les Instructions dans les Cabanes qui se trouuoient tousjours
plaines d'une grande foule de peuples, il prit resolution de parler a tous publiquement dans vne assemblée g^nale qu'il conuoqua en plaine Campagne, les
Cabanes estant trop estroites po⁹ tout le monde.   ce
fut vne belle prairie proche du bourg qu'on Choisit
pour ce grand Conseil, et qu'on orna a la facon du
païs la Couurant de nattes et de peaux d'ours, et le
p. ayant faict estendre sur des Cordes diuerses pieces
de taftas de la chine, il y atacha quatre grandes
Images de la s^te. Vierge qui estoient veües de tous
Costés.   L'auditoire estoit Composé de 500 tant de
chefs que de vieillards assis en rond a l'entour du
pere et de toute la Jeunesse qui se tenoit debout au
nombre de plus de 1500 ho^es. sans compter les femmes
et les enfans qui sont en grand nombre, le bourg
estant Compose de 5 a 600 feux.   Le pere parla a
tout le peuple, et leur porta 10 paroles par dix
presents qu'il leur fit, leur expliqua les principaux
mysteres de nostre Religion, et la fin po⁹ laquelle il
estoit veneu en leur païs; sur tout il leur precha J.
C. la veille mesme (de ce grand iour) qu'il estoit
mort en Croix, po⁹ eux aussi bien que po⁹ tout le
reste des ho^es. et dit ensuite la s^te. messe.   trois Jours
apres qui estoit le dimanche de pasques les choses
estant disposées de la mesme maniere que le Jeudy,
il celebra les s^ts. misteres po⁹ la 2de. fois Et par ces
deux sacrifices qu'on y eut iamais offerts a dieu, il
prit possession de cette terre au nom de J. C. et donna

he had occasion to suffer much, both from his own
Illness, from which he had not entirely recovered,
and from the very severe and unfavorable weather.
On at last arriving at the village, he was received
as an angel from Heaven.   After he had assembled
at various times the Chiefs of the nation, with all the
old men, that he might sow in their minds the first
seeds of the gospel, and after having given Instruction in the Cabins, which were always filled with a
great crowd of people, he resolved to address all in
public, in a general assembly which he called
together in the open Air, the Cabins being too small
to contain all the people.   It was a beautiful prairie,
close to a village, which was Selected for the great
Council; this was adorned, after the fashion of the
country, by Covering it with mats and bearskins.
Then the father, having directed them to stretch out
upon Lines several pieces of chinese taffeta, attached
to these four large Pictures of the blessed Virgin,
which were visible on all Sides.   The audience was
Composed of 500 chiefs and elders, seated in a circle
around the father, and of all the Young men, who
remained standing.   They numbered more than 1,500
men, without counting the women and children, who
are always numerous,— the village being Composed
of 5 or 600 fires.   The father addressed the whole
body of people, and conveyed to them 10 messages,
by means of ten presents which he gave them.   He
explained to them the principal mysteries of our
Religion, and the purpose that had brought him to
their country.   Above all, he preached to them Jesus
Christ, on the very eve (of that great day) on which
he had died upon the Cross for them, as well as for
all the rest of mankind; then he said holy mass.   On

a cette mission le nom de la Conception Immaculée
de la s^te. vierge.

Il fut escouté auec vne Joye vniuersselle de tous
ces peuples qui le prierent auec de tres grandes
Instances qu'il eust a reuenir au plustost chés eux
puis que sa maladie l'obligeoit a s'en retourner. Le
p. de son Costé leur tesmoigna l'affection qu'il leur
portoit la satisfaction qu'il auoit d'eux, et leur donna
parolle que luy ou vn autre de nos peres reuiendroit
po^9 Continuer cette mission si heureusement Commencée ce qu'il leur promit encore a diuerses reprises
en se separant d'auec eux. po^9 se mettre en
Chemin, ce qu'il fit auec tant de marques d'amitié de
la part de Ces bonnes gens qu'ils vouleurent l'acom-
pagner par honneur pendant plus de 30 lieues de
Chemin, se Chargans a l'enuy l'un de l'autre de son
petit bagage.

SECTION SECONDE   LE P. EST CONTRAINT DE QUITER
SA MISSION DES ILINOIS SA DERNIERE
MALADIE, SA PRETIEUSE MORT
AU MILIEU DES FORETS.

APRES que les Ilinois eurent prit Congé du pere
remplis d'une grande idée de l'euangile, il Con-
tinua son voyage et se rendit peu apres sur le lac des
Ilinois sur lequel il auoit pres de cent lieües a faire
par vne routte inconneüe a ou il n'auoit Jamais esté
parce qu'il estoit obligé de prendre du Costé du sud
de ce lac estant venue par celuy du nord. Mais
ses forces diminuerent de telle facon que ses deux
ho^es. desespererent de le porter en vie Jusqu'au
terme de leur voyage Car de fait il deuint si foible
et si espuisé qu'il ne pouuoit plus s'ayder n'y mesme

the third Day after, which was easter sunday, things
being prepared in the same manner as on Thursday,
he celebrated the holy mysteries for the 2nd time;
And by these two, the only sacrifices ever offered there
to God, he took possession of that land in the name
of Jesus Christ, and gave to that mission the name
of the Immaculate Conception of the blessed virgin.

He was listened to by all those peoples with uni-
versal Joy; and they prayed him with most earnest
Entreaty to come back to them as soon as possible,
since his sickness obliged him to return. The father,
on his Side, expressed to them the affection which
he felt for them, and the satisfaction that they had
given him; and pledged them his word that he, or
some other of our fathers would return to Carry on
that mission so happily Inaugurated. This promise
he repeated several times, while parting with them
to go upon his Way; and he set out with so many
tokens of regard on the part of Those good peoples
that, as a mark of honor they chose to escort him for
more than 30 leagues on the Road, vying with each
other in taking Charge of his slender baggage.

SECTION SECOND. THE FATHER IS COMPELLED TO
LEAVE HIS ILINOIS MISSION. HIS LAST
ILLNESS. HIS PRECIOUS DEATH IN
THE HEART OF THE FOREST.

AFTER the Ilinois, filled with great esteem for the
gospel, had taken Leave of the father, he Continued his journey, and shortly after reached the lake
of the Ilinois, upon whose waters he had to journey
nearly a hundred leagues, by an unknown route,
whereon he had Never before traveled; for he was
obliged to coast along the southern Shore of the lake,

se remuer, et il falloit le manier et le porter coe vn enfant.

Cependant il Conseruoit en cet estat vne egalité d'esprit vne resignation, vne Joye et vne douceur admirable, consolant ces chers Compagnons, et les encourageant a souffrir patiemment toutes les fatigues de ce voyage dans l'asseurance que Dieu ne les abandonneroit pas apres sa mort ; ce fut pendant cette nauigation qu'il commança a s'y preparer plus particulierement. Il s'entretenoit par diuers Colloques tantost auec nostre Seigneur tantost auec sa sacrée mere, ou auec son ange gardien ou auec tout le paradis, on l'entendoit souuent repeter s[C]es parolles, credo quod redemptor meus viuit, ou bien maria mater gratiæ, mater dei memento mei, outre sa lecture spirituelle qu'on luy faisoit tous les Jours, il pria sur la fin qu'on luy leust sa meditation de la preparation a la mort qu'il portoit sur luy, il recitoit tous les Jours son breuiare, et quoy qu'il fut si bas que sa veüe et ses forces estoit beaucoup diminuées Il ne cessa point jusqu'au dernier jour de sa vie apres que ses gens luy en eurent faict scrupule.

huit Jours auant sa mort il eut la pensée de faire de l'eau benite po⁹ luy seruir pendant le reste de sa maladie, a son agonie, et a sa sepulture, et il Instruisit ses Compagnons comment il en fa*l*loit vser.

La veille de son trepas qui fut vn vendredy il leur dit tout Joyeux que ce seroit le lendemain, il les entretint pendant tout ce Jour de ce qu'il y auoit a faire po⁹ son enterrement, de la maniere dont il faloit l'enseuellir, de la place qu'il faloit choisir po⁹ l'enterrer, comment il luy faudroit acomoder les pieds les mains, et le visage, coe ils esleueroient vne

having come by the northern.   But his strength was
so rapidly diminishing that his two men despaired of
being able to bring him alive To the end of their
journey.   Indeed, he became so feeble and exhausted
that he was unable to assist or even to move himself,
and had to be handled and carried about like a child.

Meanwhile, he Preserved in that condition an
admirable equanimity, resignation, Joy, and gentleness, consoling his dear Companions and encouraging
them to suffer patiently all the hardships of that
voyage, in the assurance that God would not abandon
them after his death.   It was during this voyage
that he began to make more special preparation for
death.   He held Communion, sometimes with our
Lord, sometimes with his holy mother, or with his
guardian angel, or with all paradise.   He was often
overheard repeating These words, *Credo quod redemptor meus vivit;* or, *maria, mater gratiæ, mater dei,
memento mei.*   In addition to the spiritual exercise,
which was read to him every Day, he requested
toward the close that they would read to him his
meditation preparatory for death, which he carried
about with him.   He recited every Day his breviary;
and although he was so low that his sight and
strength were greatly enfeebled, He continued to do
so to the last day of his life, despite the remonstrance
of his companions.

Eight Days before his death, he was thoughtful
enough to prepare the holy water for use during the
rest of his illness, in his agony, and at his burial; and
he Instructed his Companions how it should be used.

The evening before his death, which was a friday,
he told them, very Joyously, that it would take place
on the morrow.   He conversed with them during

Croix sur son tombeau Jusques la mesme qu'il les
aduertit 3 heures auant que d'expirer que si tost
qu'il seroit mort qu'ils prissent la Clochete de sa
Chapelle po⁹ la sonner pendant qu'ils le porteroient
en terre parlant de toutes ces choses auec tant de
repos et auec vne si grande presence d'esprit qu'on
eut creu qu'il s'agissoit de la mort et des funerailles
de quelq⁹ autre et non pas des siennes.

Ainsi les entretenoit il en chemin faisant sur le
lac jusqu'a ce qu'ayant aperceu vne riuiere sur le
bord de laquelle il y auoit vne eminence qu'il trou-
uoit bien propre po⁹ y estre enterré; Il leur dit que
C'estoit la le lieu de son dernier repos, ils vouleurent
pourtant passer outre parce que le temps le
permetoit, et le jour n'estoit pas aduancé mais dieu
suscita vn vent Contraire qui les obligea de retourner et entrer dans la riuiere que le p leur auoit
designée. Ils le desbarquent donc ils luy alument
vn peu de feu, ils luy dressent vne meschante Cabane
d'escorce, ils l'y couchent le moins mal qu'ils
peuuent, mais ils estoient si saisis de tristesse qu'ils
ont dit du depuis qu'ils ne scauoient presque ce
qu'ils faisoient.

Le p. estant ainsi Couché a peu pres coe sᵗ. fᵉ.
xauier, ce qu'il auoit tousjours souhaité auec tant de
passion, et se voyant seul au milieu de Ces forets,
car ses compagnons estoient ocupés a desbarquer, il
eut loisir de repeter tous les actes auxquels il s'estoit
entreteneu pendant ces derniers Jours.

Ses chers compagnons s'estans ensuite aprochés
de luy tous abatus il les Consola et leur fit esperer
que Dieu auroit soin d'eux apres sa mort, dans ces
païs nouueaux, et inconneus, Il leur donna les der-

the whole Day as to what would need to be done for
his burial: about the manner in which they should
inter him; of the spot that should be chosen for his
grave; how his feet, his hands, and his face should
be arranged; how they should erect a Cross over his
grave. He even went so Far as to counsel them, 3
hours before he expired, that as soon as he was dead
they should take the little Hand-bell of his Chapel,
and sound it while he was being put under ground.
He spoke of all these things with so great tranquil-
lity and presence of mind that one might have supposed
that he was concerned with the death and funeral of
some other person, and not with his own.

Thus did he converse with them as they made
their way upon the lake,—until, having perceived a
river, on the shore of which stood an eminence that
he deemed well suited to be the place of his inter-
ment, he told them that That was the place of his
last repose.[45] They wished, however, to proceed
farther, as the weather was favorable, and the day
was not far advanced; but God raised a Contrary
wind, which compelled them to return, and enter the
river which the father had pointed out. They accordingly brought him to the land, lighted a little fire for
him, and prepared for him a wretched Cabin of bark.
They laid him down therein, in the least uncomfort-
able way that they could; but they were so stricken
with sorrow that, as they have since said, they hardly
knew what they were doing.

The father, being thus Stretched on the ground in
much the same way as was st. francis xavier, as
he had always so passionately desired, and finding
himself alone in the midst of These forests, for his
companions were occupied with the disembarkation,

nieres Instructions, les remercia de toutes les charites
qu'ils auoient exercés en son endroit pendant tout le
voyage, leur demanda pardon des peines qu'il leur
auoit données, les chargea de demander pardon aussi
de sa part a tous nos peres et freres qui sont dans le
païs des outaoüacs, et voulut bien les disposer a rece-
uoir le sacrement de penitence, qu'il leur aministra
po⁹ la derniere fois; il leur donna aussi vn papier
dans lequel il auoit escrit toutes ses fautes depuis sa
derniere Confession po⁹ le mettre entre les mains
du p. supʳ. a fin de l'obliger a prier Dieu po⁹ luy plus
particulierement En fin il leur promit qu'il ne les
oublieroit point dans le paradis, et coe il estoit fort
Compassif sachant qu'ils estoient bien las par les
fatigues des Jours precedents, il leur ordonna d'aller
prendre vn peu de repos, les asseurant que son heure
n'estoit pas encore si proche, qu'il les esueilleroit
quand il en seroit temps; coe de fait 2 ou 3 heures
apres il les apella estant tout prest d'entrer dans
l'agonie.

quand ils furent aprochés il les embrassa encore
vne fois pendant qu'ils fondoient en larmes a ses
pieds; puis il leur demanda de l'eau benite et son
reliquaire, et ayant luy mesme osté son Crucifix qu'il
portoit tousjours pendu a son col, il le mit entre les
mains d'un de ses Compagnons le priant de le tenir
tousjours vis a vis de luy eleué deuant ses yeux et
sentant qu'il ne luy restoit que fort peu de temps a
viure, il fit vn dernier effort Joigner les mains, et
tenant tousjours les yeux. doucement attachés a son
Crucifix, il fit a haute voix sa profession de foy, et
remercia la diuine majesté de la grande grace qu'il
luy faisoit de mourir dans la Compᵉ. d'y mourir

he had leisure to repeat all the acts in which he had
continued during these last Days.

His dear companions having afterward rejoined
him, all disconsolate, he Comforted them, and inspired them with the confidence that God would take
care of them after his death, in these new and
unknown countries.   He gave them the last Instructions, thanked them for all the charities which they
had exercised in his behalf during the whole journey, and entreated pardon for the trouble that he
had given them.   He charged them to ask pardon
for him also, from all our fathers and brethren who
live in the country of the outaouacs.   Then he undertook to prepare them for the sacrament of penance,
which he administered to them for the last time.   He
gave them also a paper on which he had written all
his faults since his own last Confession, that they
might place it in the hands of the father superior,
that the latter might be enabled to pray to God for
him in a more special manner.   Finally, he promised
not to forget them in paradise.   And, as he was very
Considerate, knowing that they were much fatigued
with the hardships of the preceding Days, he bade
them go and take a little repose.   He assured them
that his hour was not yet so very near, and that he
would awaken them when the time should come —
as, in fact, 2 or 3 hours afterward he did summon
them, being ready to enter into the agony.

They drew near to him, and he embraced them
once again, while they burst into tears at his feet.
Then he asked for holy water and his reliquary; and
having himself removed his Crucifix, which he
carried always suspended round his neck, he placed
it in the hands of one of his Companions, begging

missionnaire de J. C. et sur tout d'y mourir coe il
l'auoit tousjours demandé dans vne Chetiue cabane,
au milieu des forets, et dans l'abandon de tout
secours humain.

Apres cela il se teut, s'entretenant en luy mesme
auec Dieu   il laissoit neantmoins eschaper de temps
en temps ces mots sustinuit anima mea in verbo
ejus, ou bien celles cy mater dei memento mei qui
sont les dernieres parolles qu'il prononca auant que
d'entrer dans l'agonie qui fut tousjours tres douce
et fort tranquille.

Il auoit prié ses Compagnons de le faire souuenir
quand ils le verroient près d'expirer de prononcer
souuent les noms de Jesus et de marie s'il ne le faisoit pas de luy mesme.   Ils n'y manquerent pas, et
lors qu'ils le Crurent près de passer l'un d'eux Cria
tout haut Jesvs Maria ce que le mourant repeta
distinctement et plusieurs fois et coe si a Ces noms
sacrés quelq⁹ Chose se fut presentée a luy, il leua
tout d'un Coup les yeux au dessus de son Crucifix les tenant Collés sur cest objet qu'il sembloit
regarder auec plaisir, et ainssi le visage riant
et enflamé il expira sans aucune Conueulsion, et
auec vne douceur qu'on peut apeller vn agreable
sommeil.

ses deux pauures Compagnons apres auoir verssé
bien des larmes sur son Corps, et apres l'auoir
acomodé de la maniere qu'il leur auoit prescrite le
porterent deuotement en terre sonnant la Clochete
coe il leur auoit dit, et dresserent vne grande Croix
proche de son tombeau po⁹ seruir de marque aux
passants.

Quand il fut question de s'embarquer po⁹ partir

him to hold it before his eyes. Then, feeling that
he had but a short time to live, he made a last effort,
Clasped his hands, and, with a steady and fond look
upon his Crucifix, he uttered aloud his profession of
faith, and gave thanks to the divine majesty for the
great favor which he had accorded him of dying in
the Society, of dying in it as a missionary of Jesus
Christ,— and, above all, of dying in it, as he had
always prayed, in a Wretched cabin in the midst of
the forests and bereft of all human succor.

After that, he was silent, communing within
himself with God. Nevertheless, he let escape from
time to time these words, *Sustinuit anima mea in verbo
ejus;* or these, *Mater Dei, memento mei* — which were
the last words that he uttered before entering his
agony, which was, however, very mild and peaceful.

He had prayed his Companions to put him in mind,
when they should see him about to expire, to repeat
frequently the names of Jesus and mary, if he could
not himself do so. They did as they were bidden;
and, when they Believed him to be near his end, one
of them Called aloud, " Jesus, Mary!" The dying
man repeated the words distinctly, several times;
and as if, at These sacred names, Something pre-
sented itself to him, he Suddenly raised his eyes
above his Crucifix, holding them Riveted on that
object, which he appeared to regard with pleasure.
And so, with a countenance beaming and all aglow,
he expired without any Struggle, and so gently that
it might have been regarded as a pleasant sleep.

His two poor Companions, shedding many tears
over him, composed his Body in the manner which
he had prescribed to them. Then they carried him
devoutly to burial, ringing the while the little Bell

l'un des deux qui depuis quelques Jours auoit le
Cœur tellement saisi de tristesse et si fort acablé
d'une douleur d'estomac qu'il ne pouuoit plus ny
manger n'y respirer que bien dificilement s'aduisa
pendant que l'autre preparoit toutes choses po⁹ l'em-
barquement; *s'aduisa* d'aller sur le tombeau de son
bon pere, po⁹ le prier de l'ayder au pres de la
glorieuse vierge coe il luy auoit promis ne doubtant
point qu'il ne fut dans le Ciel, il se mit donc a
genoux, faict vne Court priere et ayant pris auec
respect de la terre du sepulchre, il l'a mit sur sa
poitrine; et aussi tost son mal Cessa et sa tristesse
fut changée en vne Joye qu'il a du depuis conseruée
pendant son voyage.

SECTION 3ᴱ CE QUI S'EST PASSÉ AU TRANSPORT
DES OSSAMENS DU FEU P. MARQUETTE QUI ONT
ESTÉ RETIRÉS DU SEPULCHRE LE 19 DE
MAY 1677, QUI EST LE MESME JOUR
QU'IL MOURUT L'AN 1675.
ABREGÉ DE SES VERTUS.

DIEU n'a pas voulu permettre qu'un depost si pre-
tieux, demeurast au milieu des bois sans honneur et dans l'oubly. Les sauuages nommes Kiska-
kons qui font proffession publiq⁹ du Christianisme
depuis pres de dix ans, et qui ont esté instruit par le
p. Marquette lors qu'il demeuroit a la pointe du sᵗ.
Esprit a l'extremité du lac supʳ. ont faict leur chasse
l'hyuer passé aux enuirons du lac des Ilinois et coe
ils s'en retournoient au printemps ils furent bien aise
de passer proche le tombeau de leur bon pere qu'ils
aymoient tendrement et mesme Dieu leur donna la
pensée d'enleuer ses ossamens p⁰. les transporter en

as he had bidden them; and planted a large Cross
near to his grave, as a sign to passers-by.

When it became a question of embarking, to proceed on their journey, one of the two, who for some
Days had been so Heartsick with sorrow, and so
greatly prostrated with an internal malady, that he
could no longer eat or breathe except with difficulty,
bethought himself, while the other was making all
preparations for embarking, to visit the grave of his
good father, and ask his intercession with the glorious virgin, as he had promised, not doubting in the
least that he was in Heaven. He fell, then, upon
his knees, made a Short prayer, and having rever-
ently taken some earth from the tomb, he pressed it
to his breast. Immediately his sickness Abated, and
his sorrow was changed into a Joy which did not
forsake him during the remainder of his journey.

SECTION 3RD. WHAT OCCURRED AT THE REMOVAL
OF THE BONES OF THE LATE FATHER MARQUETTE,
WHICH WERE TAKEN FROM HIS GRAVE ON THE
19TH OF MAY, 1677, THE SAME DAY AS THAT
ON WHICH HE DIED IN THE YEAR 1675.[46]
A BRIEF SUMMARY OF HIS VIRTUES.

God did not permit that a deposit so precious
should remain in the midst of the forest, un-
honored and forgotten. The savages named Kiska-
kons, who have been making public profession of
Christianity for nearly ten years, and who were
instructed by father Marquette when he lived at the
point of st. Esprit, at the extremity of lake superior,
carried on their last winter's hunting in the vicinity
of the lake of the Ilinois. As they were returning
in the spring, they were greatly pleased to pass near

nostre Eglise de la mission de s^t. Ignace a missilima-
Kinac ou ils font leur demeure.

Ils se rendirent donc sur le lieu, et deliberent
ensemble d'agir a l'esgard du pere suiuant ce qu'ils
ont Coustume de faire enuers Ceux po^9 qui ils ont
bien du respect; Ils ouurent donc la fosse ils deue-
lopent le Corps, et quoy q^9 la Chair et les Intestins
fusent tous Consumés ils le trouuent entier sans que
la peau fut en aucune facon endomagée, ce qui n'em-
pecha pas qu'ils n'en fissent la dissection a leur
ordinaire ils lauerent les os et les exposerent au soleil
po^9 les seicher, apres quoy les ayant bien rangés
dans vne quaisse d'escorce de bouleau, ils se mirent
en chemin po^9 no^9 les aporter en nostre mission de
s^t. Ignace.

Ils estoient pres de 30 Canots qui faisoient sa conuoy auec vn tres bel ordre, il s'y trouua mesme vn
tres bon nombre d'jroquois qui s'estoient Joints a nos
sauuages algonquins po^9 faire plus d'honneur a cette
ceremonie.   quand ils aprocherent de nostre maison,
le p nouuel qui y est sup^r. fut au deuant d'eux auec
le p. piercon acompagné de ce qu'il y auoit de francois
et de sauuages, et ayant faict arrester le Conuoy, il fit
les interogations ordinaires po^9 verifier que C'estoit
veritablement le corps du p. qu'ils aportoient, et
auant que de le descendre a terre on Entonna le de
profundis a la veüe de ces 30 Canots qui estoient
tousjours a l'eau, et de tout le peuple qui estoit
a terre.   apres cela on porta le Corps a l'eglise
gardant tout ce que le rituel marque en semblables
ceremonies, il demeura exposé tout ce Jour la sous
la representation qui fut la 2de. feste de la pente-
coste 8 de Juin et le l'endemain apres qu'on luy eut

the grave of their good father, whom they tenderly
loved; and God also put it into their hearts to remove
his bones and bring them to our Church at the
mission of st. Ignace at missilimakinac, where those
savages make their abode.

They repaired, then, to the spot, and resolved
among themselves to act in regard to the father as they
are Wont to do toward Those for whom they profess
great respect. Accordingly, they opened the grave,
and uncovered the Body; and, although the Flesh
and Internal organs were all Dried up, they found
it entire, so that not even the skin was in any way
injured. This did not prevent them from proceeding to dissect it, as is their custom. They cleansed the
bones and exposed them to the sun to dry; then,
carefully laying them in a box of birch-bark, they
set out to bring them to our mission of st. Ignace.

There were nearly 30 Canoes which formed, in
excellent order, that funeral procession. There were
also a goodly number of iroquois, who United with
our algonquin savages to lend more honor to the
ceremonial. When they drew near our house,
father nouvel, who is its superior, with father piercon, went out to meet them, accompanied by the
frenchmen and savages who were there; and having
halted the Procession, he put the usual questions to
them, to make sure that It was really the father's
body which they were bringing. Before conveying it
to land, they Intoned the *de profundis* in the presence
of the 30 Canoes, which were still on the water, and
of the people who were on the shore. After that, the
Body was carried to the church, care being taken to
observe all that the ritual appoints in such ceremonies. It remained exposed under the pall, all that

rendu tous les deuoirs funebres il fut mis dans vn petit Caueau au milieu de l'eglise, ou il repose coe l'ange tutelaire de nos missions des outaouas. Les sauuages viennent prier souuent sur son tombeau et po⁹ n'en pas dire d'auantage vne jeune fille agée de 19 a 20 ans que le feu p. auoit Instruite, et qui fut baptisée l'an passé estant tombée malade et s'estant adressée au p. nouuel po⁹ estre saignée, et prendre quelques remedes le p. luy ordonna po⁹ toute medecine de venir pendant 3 Jours dire vn pater et trois aues sur le tombeau du p. marquette, ce qu'elle fit et auant le 3ᵉ Jour elle fut guerie sans saignée, et sans aucuns autres remedes.

Le p. Jaques marquette de la proᶜᵉ. de champagne, est mort a l'age de 38 ans dont il en a passé 21 en la Compagnie, scauoir 12 en france et 9 en Canada. Il fut enuoyé dans les missions des algonquins superieurs qu'on nome outaouacs, et y a trauaillé auec vn Zelle qu'on doit atendre d'un hoᵉ. qui s'est proposé sᵗ. f. xauier po⁹ le modelle de sa vie et de sa mort. Il a imité ce grand S. non seulement par la diuercité des langues barbares qu'il a aprises mais aussi par l'estendue de son Zelle qui luy a faict porter la foy Jusques a l'extremité de ce nouueau monde, et a pres de 800 lieües d'icy dans les forets ou jamais le nom de J. C. n'auoit esté anoncé.

Il a tousjours demandé a Dieu de finir sa vie dans ces laborieuses missions et de mourir au milieu des bois coe son cher sᵗ. xauier dans vn abandon gⁿᵃˡ de toutes choses. Il Interposoit tous les Jours po⁹ cela les merites de J. C. et l'interssession de la vierge Immaculée; po⁹ laquelle il auoit vne rare tendresse.

Day, which was whitsun-monday, the 8th of June;
and on the morrow, after having rendered to it all
the funeral rites, it was lowered into a small Vault in
the middle of the church, where it rests as the guardian angel of our outaouas missions. The savages
often come to pray over his tomb. Not to mention
more than this instance, a young girl, aged 19 or 20
years, whom the late father had Instructed, and who
had been baptized in the past year, fell sick, and
applied to father nouvel to be bled and to take certain remedies. The father prescribed to her, as sole
medicine, to come for 3 Days and say a *pater* and
three *ave's* at the tomb of father marquette. She
did so, and before the 3rd Day was cured, without
bleeding or any other remedies.

Father Jaques marquette, of the province of champagne, died at the age of 38 years, of which 21 were
passed in the Society — namely, 12 in france and 9
in Canada. He was sent to the missions of the upper
algonquins, who are called outaouacs; and labored
therein with the Zeal that might be expected from a
man who had proposed to himself st. francis xavier
as the model of his life and death. He resembled
that great Saint, not only in the variety of barbarian
languages which he mastered, but also by the range
of his Zeal, which made him carry the faith To the
ends of this new world, and nearly 800 leagues from
here into the forests, where the name of Jesus Christ
had never been proclaimed.

He always entreated God that he might end his
life in these laborious missions, and that, like his
dear st. xavier, he might die in the midst of the
woods, bereft of everything. Every Day, he Inter-
posed for that end both the merits of Jesus Christ

Aussi a t'il obtenu par de si puissant mediateurs ce qu'il a demandé auec tant d'instance puis qu'il a eu le bonheur de mourir coe l'apostre des Indes dans vne mechante cabane sur le riuage du lac Ilinois, abandonné de tout le monde.

Nous aurions bien de choses a dire des rares vertus de ce genereux missionnaire de son Zel/e qui luy a faict porter la foy si loing et anoncer l'euangille a tant de peuples qui nous estoient inconnus; de sa douceur qui le rendit aymable a tout le monde, et qui le faisoit tout a tous, francois auec les francois, huron auec les hurons algonquin auec les algonquins; de sa Candeur d'enfant po⁹ se descouurir a ses sup⁽ˢ⁾ et mesme a toute sorte de perssonnes auec vne jngenuité qui gagnoit tous les Cœurs; de sa Chasteté angelique; de son vnion auec Dieu continuelle.

Mais celle qui a Coe predominé, estoit vne deuotion tout a faict rare, et singuliere a la s^te vierge en particulierement enuers le mistere de son immaculée conception. Il y auoit plaisir de l'entendre parler ou prescher sur cette matiere toutes ses conuerssations et ses lettres auoient quelq⁹ chose de la s^te. vierge Immaculée, c'est ainssi qu'il la nommoit tousjours, Il a Jeuné depuis l'age de 9 ans tous les samedis, et des sa plus tendre Jeunesse, il a Commencée a dire le petit office de la Conception, Inspirant cette deuotion a tout le monde quelques mois auant sa mort il disoit tous les Jours auec ses deux ho^es. vne petite couronne de l'immaculée conception qu'il auoit inuentée de cette sorte; Apres le Credo on dit vne fois le pater et l'aué, et puis 4 fois ces parolles, aué filia dei patris aué mater filij dei, aué sponsa spiritus sancti aue templum totius trinitatis, per sanctam

and the intercession of the virgin Immaculate, for whom he entertained a singular tenderness.

Accordingly, he obtained through such powerful mediators that which he solicited with so much earnestness; since he had, like the apostle of the Indies, the happiness to die in a wretched cabin on the shore of lake Ilinois, forsaken by all the world.

We might say much of the rare virtues of this noble missionary: of his Zeal, which prompted him to carry the faith so far, and proclaim the gospel to so many peoples who were unknown to us; of his gentleness, which rendered him beloved by all, and made him all things to all men — a frenchman with the french, a huron with the hurons, an algonquin with the algonquins; of the childlike Candor with which he disclosed his heart to his superiors, and even to all kinds of persons, with an ingenuousness which won all Hearts; of his angelic Chastity; and of his uninterrupted union with God.

But that which Apparently predominated was a devotion, altogether rare and singular, to the blessed virgin, and particularly toward the mystery of her immaculate conception. It was a pleasure to hear him speak or preach on that subject. All his conversations and letters contained something about the blessed virgin Immaculate — for so he always called her. From the age of 9 years, he Fasted every saturday; and from his tenderest Youth Began to say the little office of the Conception, Inspiring every one with the same devotion. Some months before his death, he said every Day with his two men a little corona of the immaculate conception which he had devised as follows: After the Credo, there is said once the *pater* and *ave*, and then 4 times

virginitatem et immaculatam conceptionem tuam
purissima virgo emunda Cor et Carnem meam, in
nominé patris; et filij [et] spiritus sancti; et enfin le
gloria patry et le tout se repetoit trois fois.

Il n'a Jamais manqué de Dire la messe de la Conception ou du moins, l'oraison quand il l'a pû, il ne
pensoit presque a autre chose Jour et nuit, et po⁹ nous
laisser vne marque eternelle de ses sentiments il a
vouleu donner le nom de la Conception a la mission
des Ilinois.

Vne si tendre deuotion enuers la mere de Dieu
meritoit quelq⁹ grace singuliere aussi luy a t'elle
acordé la faueur qu'il luy auoit tousjours demandée
de mourir vn samedy; et ses compagnons ne doubtent
point qu'elle ne se soit faite voir a luy a l'heure de
sa mort, lors qu'apres auoir prononcé les noms de
Jesus et marie il haussa tout d'un Coup les yeux au
dessus de son Crucifix les tenant attachés sur vn
objet qu'il regardoit auec tant de plaisir, et auec
vne Joye qui paroissoit sur son visage et ils eurent
alors cette impression qu'il auoit rendu son ame entre
les mains de sa bonne mere.

Vne des dernieres lettres qu'il a escrites au p.
supʳ. des missions auant son grand voyage montre
assés qu'ils estoient ses sentiments voicy coe il la
Commence.   La Sᵗᵉ. vierge immaculée m'a obtenu la
grace d'arriuer icy en bonne santé, et dans la resolution de corespondre aux desseins que Dieu a sur moy
m'ayant destiné po⁹ le voyage du sud.   Je n'ay
point d'autre pensée sinon de faire ce que Dieu veut.
ie n'aprehende rien ny les nadoissis, ny l'abord des
nations ne m'estonne pas; de deux Choses l'une ou
Dieu me punira de mes crimes et de mes lachetes,

these words: *Ave filia Dei patris, ave mater filii Dei, ave sponsa spiritus sancti, ave templum totius trinitatis: per sanctam virginitatem et immaculatam conceptionem tuam, purissima virgo, emunda Cor et Carnem meam: in nomine patris, et filii, et spiritus sancti,*—concluding with the *gloria patri,* the whole repeated three times.

He Never failed to Say the mass of the Conception,—or, at least, when he could do so, the prayer of the Conception. He hardly meditated upon anything else Day and night. That he might leave us an ever-enduring testimony of his sentiments, it was his desire to bestow on the mission of the Ilinois the name of la Conception.

So tender a devotion toward the mother of God merited some singular grace; and she accorded him the favor that he had always requested—to die on a saturday His companions never doubted that she appeared to him at the hour of his death, when, after pronouncing the names of Jesus and mary, he Suddenly raised his eyes above his Crucifix, holding them fixed on an object which he regarded with extreme pleasure, and a Joy that showed itself upon his features; and they had, at that time, the impression that he had rendered up his soul into the hands of his good mother.

One of the last letters that he wrote to the father superior of the missions before his great voyage, is sufficient evidence that such were his sentiments. He Begins it thus: " The Blessed virgin immaculate has obtained for me the favor of reaching this place in good health, and with the resolve to correspond to the intentions which God has respecting me, since he has assigned me to the voyage toward the south. I have no other thought than that of doing what God

ou bien il me faira part de sa Croix que ie n'ay point
encore portée depuis que ie suis en ce pays icy   Mais
putestre qu'elle m'est obtenue par la s[te]. vierge immaculée ou peut estre vne mort po[9] cesser d'offencer
Dieu, cest a quoy ie tache de me tenir prest m'aban-
donnant tout a faict entre ses mains. Je prie V. R.
de ne me point oublier et de m'obtenir de Dieu
que ie ne demeure point ingrat des graces dont il
m'acabie.

on a trouué parmy les papiers vn Cahier intitulé
la Conduite de Dieu sur vn missionnaire ou il faict
voir l'excelence de cette vocation, les aduantages
qu'on y trouue po[9] s'y sanctifier et le soin que Dieu
prend des ouuriers Euangeliques, on voit dans ce
petite abregé l'esprit de Dieu dont il estoit possedé.

wills. I dread nothing — neither the nadoissis, nor the reception awaiting me among the nations, dismay me. One of two Things will happen: either God will punish me for my crimes and cowardice, or else he will give me a share in his Cross, which I have not yet carried since my arrival in this country. But this Cross has been perhaps obtained for me by the blessed virgin immaculate, or it may be death itself, that I may cease to offend God. It is that for which I try to hold myself in readiness, surrendering myself altogether into his hands. I entreat Your Reverence not to forget me, and to obtain for me of God that I may not remain ungrateful for the favors which he heaps upon me."

There was found among his papers a Manuscript entitled " The Directing care of God over a missionary," in which he shows the excellence of that vocation, the advantages which it affords for self-sanctification, and the care that God takes of Gospel laborers. One sees in this little abstract the spirit of God which possessed him.